My Life
in Poems

Darlene DeAngelis

Copyright © 2017 by Darlene DeAngelis

My Life in Poems
by Darlene DeAngelis

Printed in the United States of America.

ISBN 9781498482127

All rights reserved solely by the author. The author guarantees all contents are original and do not infringe upon the legal rights of any other person or work. No part of this book may be reproduced in any form without the permission of the author. The views expressed in this book are not necessarily those of the publisher.

www.xulonpress.com

To All of My Readers

I want to first thank God for this opportunity to speak to the world through my poetry. I want to thank my daughter Heather, my handsome grandson Kelvin Jr. and my beautiful granddaughter Amiyah, the Evans and Morris Family (My forever families), who have inspired me to do this "God assignment".

I am forever grateful for my mom and dad who are now in Heaven, who instilled in me how important it is to always believe in Jesus Christ, Father God, My Lord and Savior. Every one of my poems, has a message to tell the world. God is so amazing, what an honor and a blessing it truly is to be able to express myself through my words of poetry. We all have special gifts God has instilled within us, what is yours?

I want to thank my editor Jennifer K. from Xulon Press, who has guided me every step of the way in this process of the unknown. Lastly, to all my readers, thank you for purchasing my book. My hope is that you will find comfort in some way knowing that there is another person that may have not wore the same shoes but has walked through the same shoe store. My hearts desire, is that people who do read these poems, will know that someone other then themselves understands the heartache as well as the joy, laughter and happiness life can give to you. I pray that you can find true happiness in life and that the trials we go through can show the strength we have inside to get through.

About The Author:

My name is Darlene DeAngelis, I reside in Massachusetts. For the last 37 years I began writing poetry. This is my first book of my life experiences that tell a story in poetry form. My life has been a slow process of healing, strength and endurance. I give all the praise to God for this. As I continue to walk forward into my future, I know who is beside me guiding me, his name is Jesus. If it was not for him and my strong faith in him, I would of not made it this far in my life. For many years, I have walked through my own tunnel of darkness, and today I can now say, I am finally experiencing this light at the end of my tunnel, I call hope.

I will continue to walk forward into my future with Jesus, who is always by my side. I look back at all these years I have traveled, it has truly been amazing I consider this my own tunnel of darkness, my own life testimonies and belief, and today I can honestly say I am finally experiencing a light at the end of my tunnel, I call hope.

WORLD PEACE

Now's the time
The end is near
Listen carefully
Do you can hear
The cries of others
Beyond the grave
The killings must stop
Must go away
The living must live
Fight for what's right
Before it's to late
No world peace in sight
We need to stand up proud
We need to stand up strong
Before it all ends
To home we will go
So give it your all
Let it be known
There is no more time
Evilness needs to end

DISCONNECTED FROM GOD

What a desperate path to walk
No light for guidance
Only darkness to stumble
Valley's so deep
Mountains so tall
A burning within
Right down to the soul
Tears of sadness flow like a stream
When will it stop
Happiness a thing of my past
Families torn apart
Feeling lost
Feeling fear
Feeling need
Feeling suffering
Feeling loneliness
Feeling brokenness
Feeling hopeless
Feeling despair
Feeling anger
Feeling pain
Feeling confusion
I am tired God
Disconnected from God

IS SHE DEAD YET (PAIN OF A MOTHER)

A prodigal daughter
Missing once again
No one understands
They never walked in my shoes
They never felt my pain
They never understood why
As you continued this deadly path
Leaving the impact that shattered scattered
The ones you left your destruction with
Danger all around once again
Praying and hoping once again
Please God once again
I need you God once again
Waiting so long once again
Loosing Time once again
Wasted time once again
Anger surfaces once again
Self centeredness once again
Pain within once again
Heart broken once again
Wondering why once again
Letting you slowly go once again
Did my best once again
A pain of a mother once again

I WAIT I HOPE

About you
About me
About us
I wait I hope
The past
The present
The future
I wait I hope
The days
The weeks
The months
I wait I hope
On love
On truth
On reality
I wait I hope
On questions
On answers
On stories
I wait I hope
Do you
Will you
Can you
I wait I hope
A sign
A feeling
A direction

BROKEN SPIRIT WITHIN
(A TRIBUTE TO MY FAMILY)

Broken spirit within
Who broke you
What broke you
Hopelessness
Forced to live one more day
A while longer you say in your head
You hear pieces shattered and scattered
So many broken pieces
No need to go on
Only to let go
Days of darkness
Days of desperation
Days of suffering
Days of pain
Days of hurt
Days of anguish
Days of self hate
Indwelled spirit grieves within
Feeling everything
Once again
An emptiness that echoes so loudly
You only hear your own emptiness
No words spoken
No thoughts spoken
No signs apparent
Waiting for death
Wanting death
An acceptance within you
No thrive to live
Only thrive to die
Feeling of helplessness
Death comes
Then acceptance

BROKEN HEARTS
(A TRIBUTE TO MY MOM AND DAD)

Broken Hearts shattered and scattered about
By the many who inflicted your innocence
What broke your hearts what did it
Who broke your heart was it who did it
Your painful silence deep within
Is it shame regret your self hate
The merciless self condemnation
Congesting your hearts
Suffocating your spirits
Broken pieces of hopes
Broken pieces of dreams
Broken pieces of desires
Broken pieces of love
Broken inside
Weighing heavily on your being
Giving in
Giving up
Letting go

I DROWN

In my thoughts
My actions
My dreams
My reality
My past
My present
My future
My memories
My pain
My wishes
My desires
My love
My words
My negative
My positive
My self image
My self worth
My self love
My self hate
My confusion
My rejection
My doubt
My independence
My fear
My talents
My intelligence
My stupidity
My gullibility
My creativity
My loneliness
My strength
My weakness
My strong will

My Life in Poems

My self acceptance
My challenges
My brokenness
My compassion
My kindness
My humor
My likes
My dislikes,
My changes
My chances
My risks
My belief
My abuse
My life
My God

BREAKING INTO PIECES

Breaking into pieces
Trying to find the way back
The road so long
Emptiness is a continual void
Where the light does not exist
Where darkness consumes the light
Memories of me myself and I
Searching only to loose that feeling of touch
Echoes of silence a haunting reminder
Loosing the self to the unknown
Watching and pondering
A merry go round of confusion
Nothing seems to fill it or fit into it
A familiar voice speaks
An awareness rises up inside
Working through the edge
Desperation running from what who
Forever is a nothing to most
As the reality of it all emerges
Breaking into pieces
Once again
As this world closes in
Tosses and turns
Back forth up and down
Walking through this turmoil
It is always the same feeling of hopelessness
The same darkness surrounds the outer shell of yourself
As the head hears the voice of demise
Desperation was never left behind
Playing so loudly and violently
Trying to destroy the inside of me
Breaking into little pieces

GALLERY OF MY LIFE

Gallery of my life
A collection of images in my mind
A motion picture plays over and over and over again
They are the finest memories
Colorful pictures, dark and black all the negative ones
Spread out for all the world to see
Feel my pain you cannot see
Who I truly am no hiding place for me
One story to many stories
No one the same
Touching souls around the world
All the changes I have been through
Still standing tall and strong
No cracks no breaks just bending
Only hurts you cannot feel or see in me
Do you know me maybe
Do you want to know me, maybe
What does maybe mean to you to me
My gallery in life so much to it
Nothing seems simple
Only complicated
But who I am is so true
What you see in me, is what you get for you
Take it or leave it is all up to you
No time allowed to waste any longer for me

OCEAN OF ANGER

Was it abuse
Was it neglect
Was it secrets
Was it lies
Was it cruelty
Was it control
Was it manipulation
Was it cheating
Was it addiction
Was it injustice
Was it evilness
Was it selfishness
Was it ego
Was it pride
Was it silence
Was it greed
Was it disrespect
Was it unfaithfulness
Was it indecisiveness
Was it you

OWN YOUR OWN ALWAYS

Own your own always
Power
Liberation
Strength
I can
I will
I shall
I can
Choice
Freedom
Yes
No
Movement
Self
Thoughts
Dreams
Desires
Deeds
Love
Kindness
Compassion
Honesty
Humbleness
Happiness
Direction
Journey
Life
Truth
Voice
Opinion
Uniqueness
Contentment
Time

BROKEN CONCRETE WALL

A crack to big to mend now
Smashed into little pieces
Laying there waiting
For someone to pick up the broken pieces of me
Myself is all those broken pieces
My world disturbed once again
By the many broken pieces
On the verge of scattering
Waiting to be placed back together again
Waiting for the prepared repair
Wait I say wait
The whole pieces lay there in a pile
Altogether scattered
Small medium large some extra large
Funny thing they all look the same
My heart my feelings my being relating relentless
Of the many who smashed me into little pieces
Filled with hopes and dreams
Shattered scattered splattered
But then I begin to put it all together
So differently

My Life in Poems

LOSES TO

Accepting self
Loving life
Experiencing adventure
Taking chances
Finding your talent
Embracing challenges
Holding on to wealth
Having faith
Having Hope
Accepting Love
Knowing your Strength
Keeping your joy
Feeling your happiness
Experiencing your courage
Accepting your failures
Controlling your fears
Trusting yourself
Discovering yourself
Becoming united together
Living your dream
Always doubting
Idea's that should of been
Receiving the goodness in life
Good intentions that do not matter
Bad intentions of others
Waiting and wanting
Desiring and needing
Respect towards others
Self love and self respect
Present and future
Compassion and understanding
Embracing and touching
Feelings of acceptance

Control and reality
Speaking up and being heard
Honesty and truth
Family relationships
Living and dying
Friendships and acquaintances
Going on and staying stuck
Giving up and giving in

OUR AFFLICTED ADDICTED SELVES

Our afflicted addicted selves
Our lives covered with all this pain
Storing up all the memories
With the clutter in our minds
As life spins out of control
Covering up by pretending
The experiences in our lives covered up
By the using and abusing
Our mental and psychological wellness vanishes
It dies each minute of each day
Slowly killing ourselves
Only being haunted by our past pain
Looking back at the past in front to the future,
Never an ounce of hope to know
With the grief that eats us up inside,
The chatter in our minds,
The lies that whisper quietly
As the loudness drives us to our insanity
We are the only ones that hear it
Voices making choices in our head
Burying the bad as it rises to live
With the monsters that continue to live within us
Covering up the solitude of peace

DARKNESS

In our minds
In our spirit
In our soul
In our hearts
It consumes us each day
No relief in sight
Darkness follows us
Here there everywhere we go
It consumes us every second of every minute of each day
No rest or peace
You want to escape
You choose not to or is it just the way it is
As you try to shake it off
This thing called darkness in us
It is the evil that will not go away
Taking you down swiftly
Taking your life slowly
Give you hopelessness that never goes away
A hole inside your heart to your soul
You scream once again
You plead once again
Your complete being is half way gone
As this darkness
Continues to consume the soul of agreement

WELCOME TO THE HUMAN RACE

Where it never seems to slow down
Where fears is present in the mind
Where no one seems to care
Where families are split apart
Where beauty is inside never revealed outside
Where the truth is lies
Where deceit is necessary to survive
Where desperation seems to be the end result of suicide
Where the good old days is a craving of your past
Where no one is really accepted much
Where uncertainty is a daily dose
Where love has faded away
Where kindness has lost it's way
Where belonging is not a reality
Where loneliness seems to never go away
Where violence seems to be normal
Where God and prayer no longer exist
Where someone hates and that is ok
Where bullying is a killer
Where a voice becomes silenced
Where your pain is not my pain
Where your problem is not my problem
Where you don't care and I don't care
Where to many have an opinion you should live by
That violation is a green light in your mind
Where the world seems so much heavier to live in now
Where wondering why nothing is ok much any more
Where things that were wrong are now right
Where death is a welcoming escape

WALKING SHOES OF LIFE

Big
Small
Wide
Narrow
Smart
Stupid
Insightful
Honest
Guilty
Jealous
Evil
Mean
Gentle
Forceful
Aggressive
Passive
Slow
Fast
Analytical
Debating
Brave
Timid
Religious
Atheist
Cold
Hot
Messy
Overwhelming
Powerful
Tight
Loose
Plain
Noisy

Quiet
Talented
Rough
Sorrowful
Sensitive
Practical
Happy
Sad
Weird
Strange
Funny
Serious
Hopeful
Fat
Thin
Strong
Weak
Pretty
Generous
Confident
Angry
Beautiful
Logical
Combative
Controlling
Peaceful
Past
Present
Future
Giving
Trusting
Untrusting
Addicting
Ignorant
Inspirational

Fearful
Fearless
Joyful
Creative
GOD

BELIEVE IN PEACE

Sit awhile
Share a smile
Look at you
Look at me
We are no different
Can't you see
Your sorrow
The same as mine
Your pain
The same as mine
Your Fear
The same as mine
Just remember I am here,
You are there
I extend my hand to you

WORDS OF ACTION

Many times words unspoken
Actions are the movement to reality
It is so loud that she hears so clearly
The statements of honesty and truth
Unexpected or expected
Did it numb you
Did it make you more alive
Was your unawareness your awareness
Between a man and a woman words clearly spoken
As she quietly walks away from this man
Smiling to herself as the end comes near
Between the both of them
Lessons to be learned to be penetrated some how
As she graduates from yet another man, that entered her life
If for just a short time
The awareness to her of the unknown is before her
As she begins to embrace this new journey
With hopes that this one will be better this time around
No regrets she feels inside
Knowing she gave her all once again,
To a man who could not give to her the same
She no longer wants to forget herself
She will keep a reservation of herself
Completely to herself
Protecting what is most sacred within
A wall around her heart no longer allowing
Another break to enter it.
Her awareness will now be a mirror of her breaths
The hope one day she holds so close to herself,
Will be this man as she walks away
Leaving it all behind her
And once again he will appear in front of her
She will finally understand who she truly was

And who she truly is now
Proving the love he had for her back then
And now is ready for her hopes dreams and desires to emerge
Only to share with another one
A man she believes is the end to her searching
Only to discover the realization of the questions
That once again rise up within her
Will I or will I not

(IM)PERFECTLY POSSESSED

Can't stop
Won't stop
Feels good
Feels bad
Voices screaming inside
Do it
Don't do it
Why
Why not
Who cares
I care
I will
I won't
Hurt me
Hurt you
Pain on me
Back at you
Oh these evil thoughts
Tossed through my head
Spinning out of control
Holding onto nothing
Letting go of something
Just for that moment
(IM)perfectly possessed.

LEGENDARY SURVIVOR

Of your abuse
The burning inside of me
Is that small flame into a burning inferno
Just like it happened to us yesterday
Many years I count as void
The haunting words of your voice to me
I will haunt you till the day you die
Success has finally lost it's sting
Your words have finally died inside of you
The anger hate resentment rage inside of me
Burning into the core of my soul
Need to let go to heal to be free of you forever
Holding on tightly to God
Surrendering my control to God
As I seek gentleness onto myself
I ask why and cannot get at you
You died and I did not cry
Want to make him pay
Make him feel what he has done
Make him feel what I have felt
To a baby and young girl
Can't seem to erase you from my memory
All that you had done to us
As you slowly suffered to your death
As it matters no longer about you
Knowing what you did to us
If only for a short while
Knowing you are gone
You have truly made me
I am that legend you see
A survivor of your abuse
I am finally free

THE MEANNESS OF YOU

This is a reality of me
A true meaning of you
What I see in you
What I hear from you
What I feel about you
All these regrets I have with you
Not thinking how abnormal you were
What I allowed from the beginning to the end with you
The brokenness I felt when you had left me
What I no longer accept from you
The true realization
The best moment in my life
Loneliness that no longer haunts me
The reality that you are no longer there for me
The tears that no longer flow for you
The memory of who you truly were to me
Is what I call the disposal of you
As I pick up all the pieces of my life
And leave you far behind

THE "4" SEASONS IN LIFE

As fall fades and
And winter approaches
The realization is so clear
All things come to an end
A new beginning pleasantly appears
A life that once again needs to be lived
Settling into this change of complaining
The consistency of cold and quiet
The world in its pure nakedness
The winter makes a grand entrance into the world slowly
As the snow falls to cover us the memory of fall
With its purity of the whiteness and coldness
Falling from the sky from the clouds
As we feel and wonder if it will ever end
Then it slowly stops to the end
As we wait patiently for the next "4" seasons once again
As the world wakes up slowly from a sleep walk things to do
Coming alive steadily everyday of every hour
As the death of winter dies out once again
We the people population will once again
Wake up and live through the next "4" seasons
All over again wasting time on this beautiful time of change

GO WITH THE FLOW

Life is Life
Filled with ups and downs,
Bumpy roads
A detour or two
The punches that startle you back to reality
The hits that can knock you down
The slaps that wake you up
Only bending
Never really breaking
Living in the past
Is it the future of the past experiences you ponder
Looking back if for just a moment
Looking forward to what will be next in life
Carrying the fear
Carrying the regrets
Carrying the negative
Carrying your enemies
Loosing some friends
Wondering where compassion went
Questioning if love is real
Holding onto the hate of injustice
Keeping the anger by your side
Causes our turmoil inside
Hoping for chances
Embracing happiness every step of the way
Filling the voids
Wiping the tears of sadness away
Knowing what hope is
Living the dream that God intended for you
Feeling that desire of change
Realizing there is no unfulfillment
Forgiving your mistakes
All the lessons that are the requirement to move on
Then the completeness of self happens

TENDER HEART

You take you break it once again
Realize you do not deserve my heart
My time is precious
No more wasting it on you
I am a loser and a winner in one
Letting go of you was simple and easy
As it always has been in my life
I now realize what it was,
You were all in my head
It was never in my tender heart
I am certain the love was just a fantasy of mine
The reality is clear now
It is time to walk away from you
Taking with me the wisdom and understanding
Of my tender heart
To surround it with a protection
That yet another will never break through
To do anything less than love me sincerely

WALL OF PROTECTION

Wall of protection
A familiar part of me
Deep within me
A real love for myself
My safety place is not for you to see
As I run from you and no longer to you
Letting go with the decision of finality
Who you truly are in front of me
Just another pretend romantic love affair
As you fade to nothing in my mind
Not even a small memory now
The only regret I truly have
Is you breaking my wall of protection
As I stand in my nakedness of vulnerability
Then one day as I sit and contemplate about you
I realize now after wasted time on you
That my wall of protection
Has become stronger with resilience
And will never come down so easily again

IF ONLY FOR A MOMENT

I could breath in a new day
I could do it a new way
I could give you love freely
I could feel what you feel
It could be we and not just me
The time would stop
A year would not exist
I could bring you back
You were mine
I was yours
Life was pure happiness
You could change
I could change
I could tell you the truth
I knew your truth
I could really trust you
I could really trust me
I knew the end

MY DAILY INSPIRATIONS

My daily inspirations
Everyday will be
Seek and you will find
The Divine One who is God
He is within you within your heart and soul
Listen attentively and know he is always there
In a small voice within you
He knocks at your hearts door
He waits for you to open up the door and let him in
He sends his love and peace within you
He waits for you to pray your prayers of need
Everything from him is your blessing
What makes it sinful is our thoughts our actions
Our words and actions towards others is our karma
All of the encounters in our life can become a blessing or a curse
When you get to know who he truly is
When you being to grow spiritually
You will begin the journey of understanding him
You are the only one who can control you
Your life situations are the lessons we choose to learn
It is what you do with these situations
That will become a reality to you
Talk to Him and tell him all your troubles
He already knows all of the
H will guide you through the darkness in your life if you let him in
Always live love and laugh for tomorrow may not come
Prayer helps you through the ups and downs in your life
Grief can make you a prisoner of yourself
And what does not kill you gives you strength to go on
Freedom is a choice if you want to take it
Denial is burying the truth that needs to be revealed

My Life in Poems

Boundaries a necessary part of one's life
It is the prevention of the unnecessary suffering
Reality in life is necessary for growth

I AM YOUR MOTHER

This pain is your infliction
Filled with voids
To much lost time
Pain a friend of mine
While you go on with your life
No consideration for others
Still sitting wondering
Still sitting worrying
Still sitting pleading
Waiting for you to surrender yourself
Still sitting crying
Still sitting asking why
Sitting with my deep soul hole that echoes
Tears inside never showing outside to the world
A numbness never feeling
Letting go letting God take over you
A form of freedom,
Despair a close friend of mine
Your inflictions hit like darts
Your children suffer quietly
Finally letting go of you
Burying you in my mind daily
Not knowing the end to this nightmare
You continue to live
No one knows the pain so deep within
Rawness in the present day
Do I feel or has the numbness over taking me
You took it all away from me
You made me suffer without an ounce of shame
Never wanting to hear the reality of your cause
Eliminating the understanding of why
Never had a real acceptance of your actions and choices
Only questions echo why

Who is your blame besides you
If only you say in a mind that is blank
A million times over
Anguish anger darkness sorrow
Hopelessness helplessness despair
Want to give up want to give in
God gave you life through me
Wasting it all continually
As I sit and wait to see
Again a nothingness of your actions
Then one day a great release of peace within me
Time to let go and let God
As this reality of death will be my peace

BREAK MY HEART

As a woman
As a friend
As a person
As a wife
As a mother
As a daughter
As a sister
With your selfishness
With your foolishness
With your evil intentions
With excuses
With your self destruction
With your overdoses
With suicide
With your abuse
Wasting my time
Using me
With your anger
With your neglect
With your deception
With your children
With your actions
With your words
With your insults
With what you do
With what you do not do
With your self infliction

THE ADDICT

Do they understand
Do they care
Do they want it to stop
Do they know they are wasting their time
Do they feel
Do they know what anger is
Do they know what sorrow is
Do they know what fear is
Do they die to live or live to die
Do they know the hurt they cause others
Do they know what
Do they know when
Do they know where
Do they know how
Do they know the end
Do they know miracles
Do they know healing
Do they disconnect
Do they know the pain we feel
Do they know God
Do they know numbness
Do they know happiness
Do they know peace
Do they know time
Do they know life
Do they know the impact,
Do they know the uncertainty
Do they know how to quit
Do they wonder why
Do they know blame
Do they know guilt
Do they know to seek help
Do they believe

Do they know who they truly are
Do they know what matters in life
Do they know how to cry
Do they know the others in their lives
Do they really care
The reality is only the unknown to them

I RUN FROM YOU

I run from my past
I run from myself
I run from fear
I run from feeling
I run from abuse
I run from your cruel intentions
I run from anger
I run from the memories
I run from those voices in my head
I run from unworthiness
I run from what is not
I run from expectations
I run from selfishness
I run from insults
I run from self doubt
I run from waiting to long
I run from lies
I run from the secrets
I run forever

DEAR GOD

Thank you for another day
Thank you for showing me the way
Thank you for all the blessings you give
Thank you for this life I live
Thank you for caring ways
Thank you for the words you say
Thank you for protecting me
Thank you for setting me free
Thank you for all the lessons you teach
Thank you for the time you to preach
Thank you for all the awareness
Thank you for closing and opening up doors for me
Thank you for the peace within
Thank you for a new day I begin
Thank you for all the wisdom I have
Thank you for not giving up on me
Thank you for seeing my heart
Thank you for your unconditional love
Thank you for getting me through all the trials and tribulations
Thank you for instilling strength in me
Thank you for believing in me
Thank you for all you do for me

GOD WILL SEE US THROUGH

If you just believe
With a new day of wonder
With a new way present in front of you
All the valleys and mountains
We continue to climb in life
All the darkness we are blinded by
When confusion spins out of control
When we cannot find our way back
When all those doubts make space in your mind
When the fear we may feel is out of control
When the heaviness we carry on our shoulders
Fill like a bag of boulders
With our trials and tribulations that still exist
With all our sorrow
With all our heart ache
With all our desperation that still exists
With all the hopelessness we cannot seem to surrender
When we do not believe
When we cannot see the light at the end of the tunnel
When doom and gloom becomes a friend
With all the changes we can't seem to accept
When our emotions are over whelming
When the thought of death is near by
But then the victory comes
We all will know

WALKING IN MY PAIN

Slowly as I glide into life
Step by step
Moment by moment
Day by day
Every breath I take
Every move I make
As the years go by
The bondage consumes every thought
When exhaustion is beyond comprehension
When I cannot see
All I can do is scream
I can't go on any longer
It's poisoning my mind
It's rotting my heart
It has my soul
Does anyone care
All alone once again in my pain
As the feeling of being crushed
Consumes my entire being like a raging fire
As I wonder if anyone understands
But then I stop in the silence
With the realization once again
God is with me in my pain

NEVER

Deny yourself
Lie to yourself
Fool yourself
Disappointment yourself
Deprive yourself
Pretend who you are not
Never take less than what you give out
Be in fear of no one
Be in fear of nothing
Defend yourself
Protect yourself
Listen to negative people
Insult yourself
Not love yourself
Not be kind to yourself
Not be gentle with yourself
Not take care of yourself
Not allow love in your life
Not choosing the best for yourself
Not believing in yourself
Giving up on yourself
Stop nurturing you
Abuse yourself
Let others abuse you
Neglect what you need

DEAR GOD

I know you love me
What is unconditional love
I know you are with me
Why can't I find you
I know you know my sadness
Why don't you dry my tears
I feel so alone
Why don't I feel you near
I have so much pain
Why don't you take it all away
I don't feel you have forgiven me
When will I know
My enemies are tormenting me
Why haven't you stop them
So many people are being killed
Why haven't you protected them
There are so many in need
When will you take it away
Why haven't you helped them
I know you love us all
Why do I continue to doubt
Your presence in my life
I know you are here with me
When will I know peace completely
I feel the anger still within me
Why don't you put it out
I am bitter towards many
So many doubt your power
When will you instill belief in me
Why do so many question you
Show them who you are

BOWELS OF HELL

Self destruction of many forms
We have all been in it at times
Where the darkness
Never seems to end
Where the suffering is
Morning noon and night
Where nothing seems right and everything seems wrong
Where hope turns into hopelessness
When death is a thought that haunts you for relief
Where the pain within becomes a burning cancer
When real love turns into real hate
When you want it to end
Or you decide to end it
When you feel you are burning in the pit
All in your mind it's all in your mind
All the time every time
You no longer exist
To the reality of your life

HOPEFUL ROMANTIC

Is it giving up
Is it holding on
Is it letting go of romantic hopes
Is it getting it right
Is it getting it completely wrong
Is it going away
Is it going to stay
Is it just for one
Is it just for many
Is it a continuous yearning for something
Is it something that never seems to ever come
Is it a silence for many others
Is it only this loudness to the one who truly searches for it
Is it forever lost in the hopelessness of never happening
Is it a heartache or just an ache
Is it too much pain or just that pain
Is it to much to ask from others or to much for you
Is it the darkness or that light that shines through
Is it something lost within that you cannot fine
Is it really something to understand
Is it something to comprehend
Is it an awareness or an unawareness by choice
Is it something you continue to grab at or fear it
Is it something you cannot seem to completely touch

MASTER MY MASTER

Master my master
Where are you now
Why did you leave me
I want to do your will
Why is it so painful to live at time
I hate my sinful ways
Where has this evil darkness come from
Why are these life test so trying on me
Can you take it all away
I know you are with me always
Show me your love to me
Help me to feel your forgiveness
Are you still with me
Will you take this pain away
I ask you why continually
Not understanding your reality
I sit and cry in my sorrow and pain
I wait patiently for you
I am so lost without being found
When can I see you again
Please don't leave me
Stay close by me as you always do
So I can continue to experience
The real presence of you

SETTING ME FREE

Lord let it never end
You are truly my best friend
You always help me
So I will work for thee
To show this world who you are
Showing yourself in a mysterious knowing way
I want to thank you Lord God Jesus
For all you do once again
I want to say I love you
You are my one and only
No matter what I do
I realize within that I will always remember
You died for my sins
So I could live and love others
As you always do
And I know you live inside of me
Thank you Lord Jesus
Setting me free

I AM

The person you see
The person you talk to
The person you judge
The person you love
The person you like
The person you hate
The person you disregard
The person who accepts everyone
The person who tells the truth
The person you walk by
The person you walk with
The person who fears nothing
The person who protects
The person who is that survivor
The person who accepts challenges
The person who makes mistakes
The person who sins
The person who wants
The person who needs
The person who desires
The person who wants respect
The person who takes risks
The person who is successful
The person who isn't defeated
The person who chooses their destination
The person who never gives up
The person who never gives in
The person who is an inspiration
The person who has true happiness
The person who loves God always

LOOKING TO THE FUTURE

Looking forward forgetting the past
I eagerly wait to see
The only person standing there
Is only really me
It seems to be no different
From this thing called the past
As I wait in anticipation
With the hopes of love and family at last
Looking to the future
Is like looking at the past
Loneliness, sadness never going away
Looking to the future
The anticipation of holidays
Makes me realize one thing
No one cares except for God
As I spend them all alone,
No one makes me feel
I am good enough
One thing that is definite about me
I do care and I will always be there for you

MAYBE

For a while
I will just pass by
I won't
I'll quit
I'll loose my sense of reality
I'll forget all this familiarity
Evil will become a thing of the past
I'm out of order
I'm beginning to heal
I'M spiritually growing now
Death is only a thought
Being uncomfortable is what I need
Change is a desperate need
The suffering of your silence is just another lonely journey
My loved ones are happy now
The pain of loosing someone is not really the pain
My hunger is not the food I eat
My acceptance is not really my acceptance
My dreams are my stories of truth
My feelings are not my emotions of reality
My hurt is the afflictions of your pain
My final desire at the end is give it all to God

IS GOD REAL

You ask and wait
Is God there for me
Is my pain something to hold onto
Then a new day dawns
An incredible growth spurt of freedom
You are being stretched to go on
You resist and fight with the unknown of fear
Then all pain releases and a calmness comes
The big becomes small with what no longer matters
The signs come in from God loudly but quiet enough
You cry out in pain another sign appears in front of you
As you choose to release it
It is your loved ones
Those entities of light that come to visit
When the presence of those are here to guide us along the way
Giving you the strength and courage you need so much
Go on go forward to the mystery of the future in front of you
As you continue to question inside you mind
With so many of the signs
That you choose to ignore

LOSSES

I've had a few
Some necessary
Some needed
Some left me numb inside
Sitting and wondering why
Life has been the chosen one for me
Counting the ones that were a blessing
Feeling heartache with some
What a relief from this pain
None of them compare
None of them the same
Just different in a way
Nothing will ever be like Jesus who bears our sin
The pain and sorrow that I may feel
The despair and hopelessness in my emotions
The tears I cry
For the ones no longer here
The loved ones gone away but not forever
So when I'm tired and lonely
And I think about all of my losses
I come back to what I know
No matter what my losses are
They will come to my elimination eventually

MY LORD MY GOD

I am going to walk and talk with you
Each and everyday
Ask you to show me the way
Tell you all my sorrows and pain
Tell you all my concerns and uncertainties
Knowing that you know me completely
You are my strength within
I know my soul is strong because of you.
My tears will fall as you dry them up
I will stand up and never give up
I will try once again with you by my side
No matter what the enemy tells me what he will do
I will look up and hear you
I know you will be there to carry me, through
You will break down my walls one at a time
Helping me up when I fall
Knowing how much you love me unconditionally
Will help me fight a battle within

Reflections

Reflections
Every part of my life
Glimmers of hope
Never the same
With necessary change
Always new
Somewhat old
The ups
The downs
The future of uncertainty
Turning only to God for guidance
The reassuring voice within me
Sometimes loud
Sometimes silent
Wondering why
Wondering how
Wondering when
Wondering where
Once again
All over again
A mirror of the same reflection
Called life

JESUS

Jesus
How I love you
Each and everyday
You are always there beside me
Showing me the way
You will always be my Savior
You will always be my Lord
Your spirit lives in side of me
No matter how far I am from you
An awareness of your presence engulfs me
You speak in a voice of whispers
In to my ears
Loud enough for me to hear you
I know in my heart you love me so much
When I need you
I will call you and then you appear
I can just call out your name
You calm my inner turmoil
From all the years of pain
I realize the realness of you
Jesus how I love you
You will always be the same

FORGIVING YOU

Forgiving you was unlike my wishes
It was such a difficult thing to do
Knowing I had to
Knowing I had to free myself from your prison
It seemed not right to do
Holding that resentment and bitterness
Was a sweet revenge to me
It reminded me how much my level anger rose
It was like standing on my head forever,
It was like holding nothing that was there but emptiness
It was like eating poison waiting for you to die
But the only one who was dying was me to you
It was like never taking a breath forever
Suffocating on my own anger on you
My bleeding heart breaking into many pieces
Pulling each strand of my hair out one by one
Walking barefoot on hot coals that burn with fire
Pinching myself until it becomes numb
Biting my tongue off
Putting a nail through my hand
Taking a razor blade and slicing my lip
This is how it feels
Trying to forgive you
As I finally free myself from you prison

MY FRIEND JADE

You shared your Jade with me
Each day I went to see her
She shared herself so freely with me
She brightened my days when I was down
She was the sunshine part of my life
A beautiful dog so full of love to give
She sat at the door waiting and watching
For a sign that I would be there
Now the void is within me
Because she died last night
The kisses she freely gave to me
Will be burned in my memory forever
Jade will hold a very special place in my heart
That she is now in a special place
She is now in a very special place
Where no pain resides
As she plays and runs over the bridge of heaven with her friends
She will miss everyone she gave love to on earth
But watches over the people that loved her so very much
I saw the special family you were to Jade
If she could of spoke your language you would of known
When God picked her for your family
He knew exactly the perfect dog was her
Thank you for sharing your dog with me
She will always be in my heart

THE END TO MYSELF

The end to myself
It is finally here coming to me
All this despair
And all this pain within
Were the lessons I needed to learn
The consisted of all the violations of others
That no longer exist in my memory
Letting go was the sweetest revenge I know
God has taken away the bad
And has replaced it with his good
God knows the many inflictions upon me by others
I use to be the old me
I am now embracing the new me
Surrendering all my fears
As they tried to take me down so many times
God never let me go
Throughout this painful journey
I use to go and do it my way
I use to try to make it my way
I use to try to do it your way
I use to try to prove I was someone you made me
I finally woke up to who my true self is
I'm no longer looking back only in front of me
Knowing in my heart how I have changed
With the help from my loving God
Telling the world how I made it
Releasing finally

WHY CAN'T I BE

Why can't I be
The woman God wants me to be
Why do I struggle so much
Inside of me a war rages
Outside the calm appears
The anger and resentment
The evil intentions of others
I can't stand it anymore
I ask God to take it all away
He does not answer me
I want it all to go away
Never to come back this way
My life feels like a rollercoaster
Of ups and downs
I plummet deep within the valley of darkness
Holding on to God so tights
As the storms of life come in so strong
I want to give up
I do not accept the way my life appears
I've been through so much
The people never stop
As I fight this fight,
You torment me with your evil intentions
You abuse me so softly
I wait for your ignorance to inflict you with suffering
As I walk away with the peace I have left inside of me
Knowing that I am different now
And to finally be the woman God wants me to be

BACK TO MYSELF

Caring for you a grown man of sorts
Or this is what I thought
To me the love has arrived once again
As you quietly crept yourself near me.
A relationship before you
A mess of dysfunction and abuse you bring with you
Hiding behind that oh so perfect self
A lonely woman not seeking another significant other in life
Then poof you magically make it seem somewhat relieving to me
With so many secrets of selfish motives
Those evil intentions of self gratification only for you
A few positives I begin to see but decide to ignore
A mountain of negative baggage you carry in life
As I realize once again the same lessons
That I never learned before you
As I dig my way out
Making the piles of you look differently
I go on again with another man
All the same game of blame onto me
Just a mere man you teach me so well
Like a lemon oh so sour, sweet like sugar
A burning desire that was destroying me once again inside
Slowly breaking away from your dysfunctions
You attempt to inflict me with
A promise to myself long ago
Never again on this merry go round to no where
One day a great push within came
Just in time for me
Awaking a different woman with an awareness like a lion
Loudly screaming inside of me
Then her voice appears on the phone
Telling you what you wanted to hear
To fulfill your evil flesh and loins

Position better than the night before
Then out of guilt you call me
Tell me the love you have for me
With excitement in your playing fake voice
This dirty little porn movie playing in my mind
The two or you having sexual work to do
My mind spinning in circles
Becoming euphoric with happiness and relief
Your flesh her flesh impresses me not
Then a second of anger and despair
Left so quickly as fast as it came to me
A great relief as the words of my mouth yell out success of freedom is now mine
As I go along thinking to myself
Another wonderful life lesson others see as pain
And as for me only gain
As a deep voice inside of me yells loud and clear
It is now time for you to graduate
From this classroom of hard lessons
The teacher, was my inner voice
The Holy Spirit I know so well
Who loved me and saved me
Again from myself
Attempting to get my attention once again
I now realize how swiftly my life is going by
Leaving this behind with a sigh of relief
The memories will always be there to remind me
Of what was and never will be again
Learning to never go back
To always go forward
To one of the better classrooms of life
Knowing I am closer to my real prince charming my love and soul mate
No longer wanting to settle for less than what I give
Walking towards the new road with out you

CHRISTMAS MEMORIES

The snow is falling the world at peace
As the celebration of Jesus birth is near
Families gather from far and near
Catching up on lost times in their lives
The tree aglow with many lights
Many ornaments displayed so perfectly
Lights on the tree shimmering so brightly
The many ornaments displayed so perfectly
For all to experience for all to see
Abundant amounts of gifts placed perfectly under the tree
Pretty paper with beautiful bows cover them
Children running and playing throughout their home
Waiting eagerly for Santa's arrival
No sleep in their eyes no rest in their souls
The entrance to your home filled with the many smells you cherish
Lingers throughout the house from the kitchen
By the many foods being prepared with much love and care
As people unwind from the many days of running here and there
As they prepare once again a perfect Christmas for all to share
Now that Christmas has come and gone once again
Another year coming to a close
The many memories a book of pictures that tell a story
A thought and conversation of the past gone by
A hearts desire a smile of gratitude
If only for a moment in your life
Of a family complete on this special day we call Christmas
As we celebrate Christmas each year
We should stop and reflect
How Blessed we are by God in our lives
The love he continues to give after Christmas is gone
Reflecting on what is truly most import and simple in life

And about the Christmas of past and present
Giving away what is freely given to us from God
Gathering at church to worship God's son Jesus Christ and his birth
Love kindness a meal to share with all who is present
On this special day we share with others we love
Remembering all who have passed on to be with our Lord
Including all the memories that shall last a lifetime

I WISH YOU
(Dedication to my family and friends)

I wish you happiness
When sadness is present
I wish you light
For the darkness in your life
I wish you laughter
When you cry
I wish you peace
When your soul is restless
I wish you blessings
When times are scarce
I wish you joy
When your time has sorrow
I wish you comfort
In times of loneliness
I wish rainbows
When it rains
I wish you wisdom
When you feel lost
I wish you strength
When you feel weak
I wish you serenity
When you have no peace
I wish you courage
When fear is near
I wish you love
From God above

MY LORD MY GOD

I am going to walk and talk to you God everyday
Ask you to show me your way
Give me strength within
To know you are with me always
You will make my soul strong once again
My tears will fall and you will dry them up
I will get up as you help me and try once more
No matter what the enemy says
I will shun him away
As the protection surrounds me
From the evilness of the world
As God continues to forgive me
With his continual unconditional love
Breaking down all my walls
To be born again anew
I love you God
This is all for you

MY FAMILY

There comes a time in one's life
When you can only wonder
As you ask yourself
Are they my Family
Will they ever come back
And the only thing you can do
Is continue to look out into this dark cold world
So emotionless forgetting what to feel now
So many that live with this void
As you ask once again
Does anyone care to be my family
As you search for the right one
Only to pass by many
To love to laugh to hold onto
I pray wonder wish and hope
That God hears me
To what I miss the most
I have longed for a family for so long
As time goes by and many tears still fall
There is only the disappointment once again
A decision that others choose
Again God knows my heart so perfectly
It has been such long time
That anyone really belonged
To the reality of a my family
I was born into
I ask did they really care
As the loneliness surrounds me without that loving family
Sadness and heart ache never goes away
It stays within my heart everyday
Then one day it all changes
Your hopes dreams and desires
Through your prayers is the reality of God

A family you have waited for has returned in a different way
As they stand in front of you with their eyes filled with tears
And their arms open with love
This new life has changed suddenly
With the happiness and joy over flowing
The search is finally over
A family that will never be the same
A healing has just begun
No one but God has placed them finally back where they belong
I have finally won the family that once was lost
All the hugs and kisses of catching up
From all those lost years gone by
The sweet words you finally here welcome home so loud so clear
As the realization of being her is a true reality to each one
As God changed it all his way
That all those years just seem like yesterday to me,
That is why it is said
God has no time limit in doing things
As he smiles and shines down on us
Giving us yet another blessing in our life called Family
giving him all the glory for what he did
Speaking the words for all to hear
This family that has returned this way
Lets waste no more time
We have finally arrived back together once again
Never wanting to look back
Always wanting to look forward
Holding all the hands that were open and empty
Wondering why there were so many lost years without them
But only feeling the blessings God has done once again
With a grateful heart over flowing with happiness and love
Telling each other do not go ever again
Experiencing those complete word of family

With the love you have so much for each one
As I only ask this one thing from you
With so much love in my heart for you
Never leave again only promise to stay forever

SHINING STAR

A shining star
That is what you are
Your caring ways
Helps fill lonely days
Your kind words
Calms the soul
Your smile so bright
It makes each day so right
You are very special to many
One of a kind
Spreading happiness to a hurting world
Never giving up
So please remember this
When your life gets hard
And the darkness comes to make it presence known to you
As Despair appears to be your only friend
I am here, to be your shining star
Always know I really care about you

TRUST IN THE LORD

Trust in the lord
For God is good
He instructs my life
The way it should be
He loves me unconditionally
This I know
He protects me
Where ever I go
Every trial and tribulation
That inflicts my life
He lets me know he is always there
He gives me direction
His guidance and wisdom is so very complete
He protects each step I take
So when I call on him
I know for sure
There is this small voice
That speaks to me
Hoping I will always listen to his ways

THE LORD

The lord has been with me
All the days of my life
As he waits so patiently
To guide me
To show me,
To keep me safe everyday.
God says to me
In my silent times
I am here for you
I will never leave you
My arms are extended and open wide
Waiting to hold you and to love you
I hear your cries
Your hopes dreams and desires
Your pain I feel it more
I will fill you every need
So remember I am here close by
To guide your every step you take
I will keep you heart in a safe place from hurt
I am the only one who knows you completely
I will be there anytime you call on me
And when your life seems to be falling apart
I will pick up the pieces a of your broken heart
I promise it will be brand new
As I gently pick you up and carry you even farther in life
For I will be your everything
If you only allow me

CROSSING LIGHT

As I sit and wait
For this crossing light to change
From red to green
There appears to be something odd
But so familiar to me
The numbers on the crossing light
Go slowly down from 20 to 1
But no one is in sight
Crossing towards the light to the other side with us
Salem Massachusetts is a funny town
Many of the souls we do not see continue to live on
As they pass onto the other side we call street
Their presence on this earth
Are the many times they share
With the ones who are aware
Of the many times they have no need to rush
It is truly sad we the living people
Have not an awareness of this
As they continue to attempt to get our attention
Not a sign in sights except for this red crossing light
As we wait and wonder
We are the ones who have an awareness of this
Noticing something that catches my attention
Of the many who continue to miss the moment
Of the signs and wonders
Of these unsettled soul walking across onto the other side called street
They scream so loudly that only silence is the thing you hear
Unsettled souls talking to many only few hear them
Hello there I am here still you are there
And the ones who are aware know
Of the reality of those who are no longer here
As they say you can no longer see me this I know

But I can see you so clearly in front of me
I am beyond this place called earth
Where I once lived but I am still not too far away
I am so close to you I can touch you but you do not feel
It truly is so wonderful that you are aware I am here
As this red light turns green once again
I once again drive on
With the familiarity of knowing once again
Another kindred spirit lives on
For all who believe

PAIN

If I could take your pain away
Each and everyday
I would place it in a jar
And throw it all away
Since I cannot do that for you
I only ask this one thing of you
Forgive me if you can
Know I am sorry for all that I did
As time goes by,
And your hurt is finally leaving
I just ask you
To never stop believing
The deep sorrow and shame I feel
For what I did
Life will never be the same
My awareness of pain consumes me
Change will never make it right
The lesson I have learned is only regret
Please forgive me
One last time

POOR LITTLE CHILD OF MINE

There you are once again
This child of mine
I try to get your attention
To sit for a while with me
I see this world is heavy on you
Your soul is troubled
Your heart is broken your spirit crushed
I try to get your attention
But all you do is pass me by
I wait patiently for you
As you continue to suffer unnecessarily
So I wait patiently for you
To let you know I am the one who carries your burdens
When you feel there is no relief in sight
I whisper softly in your ear
I send people so you will hear me
Hoping you will realize
I am not far away I am close enough to you
In all that you do each and everyday
I want you to know how much I love you my child
That I hear your cries
I know your life of pain you hold onto
I ask you to fully trust in me to never fear
I will never let you go
You will always be a part of me
When things go wrong
It turns into we
I will take all your problems and pain
Throw it all away once again
One day in your life,
You will look back and see it was me when you look back to see
Who took all your pain away
So please never forget

The love I will always have for you
No matter what happens
I will make you new
As God begins to speak with me with his small voice within me
As he say to me satan has vanished can't you see
I love you so much I will never leave
He embraces me with his love
His protection is always here
As I sit and wonder how powerful God is
I know in my heart I am one of the Kings Kids
That satan will never touch me
Then the worries and fear all disappear
As God speaks to me once again
Do not ever worry my child
You have a life to live
So go on your way the devil I've killed
Be not concerned with your life
The blessings I have for you
Will be many not few
As I walked away with a smile on my face
A happiness in my heart
For at that moment I knew God spoke to me
My child we will never be apart

SATAN THE LIAR

Satan said to me
Your days are few
Can't you see
As I prayed and waited patiently
For God to appear
So I sat quietly and wondered why
The tears began to flow from my eyes
As I sat and cried
Engulfed in my fear
God came to me
And made me hear these words
Vanish satan you evil imp
You were never welcome satan say goodbye
All you do is lie
Then God took me in his loving arms
Saying these words to me
Don't you worry
Don't you cry my child
You are finally free
Now go live your life
You have much work to do for me
I give you plenty of time
To do what you need to do
So go on your way my child
Be not concerned ever again
The plans I have for you
Will be the perfect ones for you
So then I sat with a smile in my heart
Knowing no matter what satan says or does
I am with God and never apart

FADING

Fading from my memory
Fading far away from me
Wasted dreams
Wasted time
Wasted emotions all on you
What we had
Was not good
Was terrible bad
Fading from my memory
Fading far away from me
All the times you inflicted me with pain
Always wanting to take me down
Into a hole of darkness
Fading from my memory
Fading far away from me
Now I walk away you
Final free away from you
Fading from my memory
Fading far away from me
Anything to do with we
Is no longer something I need
Fading from my memory,
Fading far away from me.

FACES OF AMERICA

We are the many
We are the shapes
We are the sizes
We are the colors
We are the cultures
We are the nationalities
We are happy
We are evil
We are sad
We are poverty
We are rich
We are unsatisfied
We are oppressed
We are confused
We are loneliness
We are angry
We are fear
We are war
We are prejudice
We are labels
We are opinions
We are enemies
We are misery
We are peace
We are envy
We are greed
We are honest
We are regret
We are guilt
We are lost
We are found,
We are struggling
We are greed

We are love
We are passion
We are conditioned
We are unconditional
We are awareness
We are peace
We are all God's children

SHOULD OF
(A TRIBUTE TO MY MOM
AND DAD)

I should of done better
I should of given you more love
I should of shown you respect always
I should of given you the support that you needed
I should of talked to you more
I should of gotten to know you better
I should of understood you a lot more
I should of helped you more
I should of been there for you always
I should of given you more of my time
I should of prayed with you everyday
I should of hugged you
I should of given you kisses
I should of given you words of encouragement
I should of supported you
I should of given more of me to you
I should of not had any regrets
I should of asked for forgiveness
I should of not been impatient
I should of understood your internal pain
I should of understood your regrets
I should of understood all your pain
I should of understood your desperation
I should of understood your cries for help in silence
I wish I could have you back

WHAT AM I LOOSING

My life journey
My intelligence
My Uniqueness
My inner beauty
My outer beauty
My self image
My true self
My friendliness
My patience
My kindness
My understanding
My compassion
My trust
My honesty
My sense of humor
My intuition
My self control
My opinions
My emotions
My tears
My smile
My awareness
My protection
My brokenness
My life lessons
My regrets
My resentment
My wishes
My demands
My expectations
My fear
My concerns
My innocence

My hopes
My dreams
My voice
My dis-ease
My sickness
My faith
My belief
My afflictions
My toleration
My safety
My words
My ego
My pride
My want to try
My ideas
My inner voice
My feelings
My thoughts
My wants
My needs
My desires
My spirit
My love
My lust
My sin
My blessings
My soul
My heart
My integrity
My truth
My was
My was not
My never will be
My experiences
My lessons

My Life in Poems

My commonsense
My life path
My enemies
My clutter
My time on you
My last breath
My inner child
My wanting to play
My self doubt
My sincerity
My anger
My can
My can't
My will not
My mental stability
My true self

I WAIT

For you
For us
To know
To feel
To hear the word love
To hear your voice
To be yours
To be together
To hold your hand
To hug you
To kiss you
To spend time with you
To laugh with you
To cry with you
To walk with you
To run with you
To feel your sincerity
For you to make the first move
To feel the excitement with you
To feel total happiness with you
For my hopes to be fulfilled by you
For the dreams to become my reality with you
For my desires to come to fruition with you
For my completeness with you
For the reality of us
For your honesty with me

MR. OLD TREE

He stands in silence
Can you not see me
Can you not hear me
So many times I have spoke
Hello world I am here world
So many years have passed me by
Can't you see do you know
Who I am as you go by me
I hope you know this reality of me
I have seen so many days go by
I have weathered many storms
Mr. Sun has dried me out so much
As I stand and wait as many pass me by
I am here you are there
I am so lonely don't you know
Can't you hear my cries of desperation
Just look at me I am barely alive
As I hold my weary limbs up high
To give the animals a safe place to call home
I have become so brittle
The scales are now wearing on my outer shell
That really hurt me now
I have seen so much
I have felt so much
I have ingested so much
I have done so much
It has become apparent to me now
That all those years
And all the negativity of this world
Makes me want to scream
It is time to cut me down
Help me to finally say goodbye
It's time to leave this world

I will miss you
But the time has come
Would you please put me to rest
I have done my job for many

THE THINGZ'S

The thingz's that satisfy
The thingz that create a void within
The thingz's that make you smile
The thingz's that make you cry
The things's that make you fear
The thingz's lift your spirits
The thingz's that warm your heart
The thingz that infect world
The thingz's that invade our space
The thingz's that waste our time
The thingz's that hurt us
The thingz's that leaves you feeling emptiness
The thingz's that pollute the air we all breath
The thingz's that are ok without your consent
The thingz's that seem funny
The thingz's that seem sad
The thingz's that make you mad
The thingz's that your thoughts cause
The thingz's that people do to you
The thingz's that are unfair
The thingz's that matter the most
The thingz's you do not comprehend
The thingz's you wish you did not experience
The thingz's that clutter your thinking
The thingz's that negative words create
The thingz's that positive words create
The thingz's that change can make
The thingz's that are labeled
The thingz's that hurts your heart
The thingz's that war has caused
The thingz's that have no significance
The thingz's that lack knowledge
The thingz's of self destruction

The thingz's that self hate
The thingz's depression cause
The thingz's we hold onto
The thingz's of letting go
The thingz's we know that matter
The thingz's of shapes
The thingz's of sizes
The thingz's we give to others
The thingz's that impact us
The thingz's when life ends
The thingz's of deep regrets
The thingz's of should of
The thingz's of would of
The thingz's of could of
The thingz's of procrastination
The thingz's of the intuition
The thingz's we question
The thingz's to the future
The thingz's to the unknown
The thingz's of life
The thingz's of death
The thingz's that excite us
The thingz's that disappoint us
The thingz's that people assume about you
The thingz's to love
The thingz's to lust
The thingz's of the flesh
The thingz's that are losses
The thingz's of courage
The thingz's of wants
The thingz's of needs
The thingz's of desires
The thingz's of the devil
The thingz's that are gone for good
The thingz's affairs cause

The thingz's no tolerance creates
The thingz's that bullying cause
The thingz's suicide can do to other
The thingz's that take you away from God
The thingz's that drive you crazy
The thingz's that make you want to forget
The thingz's we need to heal from
The thingz's holding a grudge doesn't do
The thingz's holding onto hate creates
The thingz's words can impact

DEAR GOD

Why does life have to be so hard at times
Why does life have to be so painful at times
Why are so many families torn apart
Why are babies dying
Why is the government not doing their job
Why is there so much hate
Why is there so much bullying by others
Why do so many not believe in God
Why do so many blame you God
Why won't you control the free will of people now
Why do people do the same things all over again
Why is there so much violence in the world
Why can't people just love one another
Why can't we just live in peace now
Why are so many innocent people dying
Why are there so many broken families
Why are there so many broken dreams
Why are there so many broken people
Why are married people strangers to one another
Why are there so many broken marriages
Why is there so much abuse
Why are there so many broken hearts
Why are there so many hurtful words from others
Why is there so much desperation
Why is there so much suicide
Why is the human race so messed up
Why God why

WAS IT TO SOON

We ask our self was this time right on time
We wonder why they had to leave
We contemplate if they see you now
We wonder if they can hear you now
When you talk to them in silence
As we wait for what seems an eternity
For a sign for them to appear in your dreams
Missing their voice
Missing their words
Missing their embrace
Wondering if they miss you
We now question God's timing and reason
Why you were taken away from me way to soon
Many questions unanswered
Many regret that haunt you with a thought or a word of familiarity
As we hold onto them tightly in your heart
Trying to imagine where they are now
What the other side consists of
What they are doing now
We can only anticipate
We can only imagine
How they wait for us
On this unknown other side
Where we can only imagine
When we can only know
Their days away from us are so different now
While we still continue to exist on earth still here on earth
We try to believe after this love
We only hope there will be pure love
We only hope that there will be pure happiness
As God embraces us with his comforting love God
Just the way God truly is

And when the pain and sadness
Engulfs our entire being
We can be sure that the people we loved and still do
The ones we feel were taken to soon
Will be waiting for us to come home
Embracing us with their love
As they let us know how much they missed us

YOU DIED TODAY

Your presence stills stands in front of me
But today your true outer shell no longer exists to me
As you left me behind today
A piece of my heart went with you today
In a world that can be emotionless
In a world that can be so lonely without you
I died inside today
I cried for you today
Were you happy to see one another
Did you embrace one another at the end of the tunnel
Now I sit and wonder
With the void I walk with everyday
The loneliness I feel since you left me behind
Thoughts of you flood my mind
It was a blink of an eye a moment in time
You were gone from me
Now you are so far from me
No longer near to me
Living in Heaven with God now
Are you resting in peace now
With no suffering
Trouble sorrow and sickness no longer exist
Are you whole and complete now
Unlike the brokenness you experienced here
You are now mended perfectly together now
I know you are laughing with God each day
Which makes my heart filled with happiness
I continue to love the people
Who are now departed from me
One day I will see you and be with you once again
Knowing this time has gone by so quickly
With all who I have loved and lost
And with this awareness that you will guide me through
The tunnel into your paradise called home in heaven

THE GREAT (AM)

When your days are dark
And desperation is the only thing you know
Get on those knees to God
And pray each and everyday
Do not cease to believe
Continue to know God will guide you on
So keep on going
For God is all knowing
He hears our cries
Knows all our pain
There is nothing to loose
God is all that you gain
Blessed be the name
In all the earth
For he is God
And we are not

WAITING AT THE WINDOW

Waiting and wanting
That is all I know
As I anticipate your arrival
Can't you see
I use to be just like you
As I see you looking at me
There you are here I am
The only thing between us
Is this window it is a stranger but my friend.
As my life slowly fades away from me
I sit in this new home just for me
It is the neighborhood nursing home facility
That cares for me, just a little bit
As I wait patiently for my family to come be with me
Sometimes it seems no one wants to say hello
Ask me how I am
But my reality is this
No one here wants to get to know me
No one here wants to hear my stories
No one here wants to spend some time with me
Not even the people that are my family.
So days go bye as I patiently wait
I feel so sad I want to cry
So I stand at this window
Looking at everyone go by
Then I stop and see you are looking at me
But then I see you walk away from me
As I go back to my loneliness and broken heart
A familiar friend of mine
Behind the only things that separates us
Is what I know
It is called my window
With just me

DEAR SELF

A love letter finally to me
It's has been such a long time self
I forgot who you were self
I forgot how much I missed you self
I forgot how much I needed you self
I forgot that time is running out on you self
I forgot how to live with myself
I forgot how beautiful you truly are self
I forgot how loving you truly are self
I forgot how much you have given away to others self
I forgot how care for myself
I forgot how much I have lost in our life self
I forgot to spend time with my self
I forgot to get to know you self
I forgot how much you mean to self
I forgot what my true role is self
I forgot how much I have been through with you self
I forgot how much confidence has been missing in my self
I forgot how to relate to my self
I forgot how much doubt I talked into you self
I forgot all the times you turned against my self
I forgot to tell you self
Thank you for always being with me
For all you have survived with me
And now it is me and you self together again

MY TIME HAS COME

Something has made it's way to me
It is the end to the old familiar
The newness of the beginning
Just for me to enjoy
As I anticipate and wait
For the many doors that God will open just for me
So many choices with so many decisions just for me
The right ones the wrong ones
The past present and future
I will embrace it
And then sit and contemplate it all
My life such a familiar state
The old me has gone, the new me is here
My days will seem somewhat different
Only for a short while
As I walk freely now
With a fulfillment right on time
Without any limits just freedom
I have come to this realization
What the true meaning of happiness is to me
It will be my reality with an awareness
Never will ever be a stranger to me
That will lay dormant within me
I will bring it up and out of me
With a feeling of ecstatic delight within me
finally being true to me
Revealing to this world who I am and what I know
Shouting loud shouting clear for all the world to hear
The impact I will leave others
Will truly be mine and mine only
They are called the Special Footprints on this life journey
That have made their home on the hearts of many
And the ones who took the time to know me

Will be the one's who truly knew who I was
For my God has loved me so very much
Has finally open this door of success for me
Speaking in a loving voice to me
Go forward my child and touch the world
For this is your time to shine

My Life in Poems

I WAIT FOR YOU

Life rushes by
For my phone to ring
To hear your voice
To hear the words I long to hear
Saying that you love me
Saying you miss me
Saying you want me for your own
That you want to be with me
That you want to hold me
I will be your one and only
How much you adore me
That I mean the world to you
Then I see the true reality
That stands in front of me
Your cruel ways towards me
With your intentions to hurt me
That all you are is my imagination
Your words that cut so deep
Your actions are emptiness
The pain and hurt that latches onto me
Trying to understand why
Wishing you were different
Than what you are to me
You have hit me like a brick
As I spin out of control
Then it all stops so abruptly
As I sit and wish you were different
The realization of you the one who does not care
The selfishness of your gratification
That you never wanted me
Now is my time to go

LOSS OF SELF

Why did this happen to me
Why did I go away from me
Why did I give freely to others and not to me
Why did I forget about me
Why did I continue to allow this to happen to me
Why can't I find me
Why did I loose me
Why did I settle for less with me
Why could I not love me completely
Why didn't I put myself first
Why did I put myself last
Why did I forget my true meaning
Why did I hide myself to the world
Why did I run so many times from me
Why did I torture myself so much
Why did I hate myself so many times
Why did I hold onto the past and forget to live in the present
Why didn't I respect me fully
Why did I loose me along the way

I AM OK

There is nothing more for you from me
No longer wanting to keep you happy and make stay
To lie to you and tell you I still care
When my emotions are not there
To know in my heart
My happiness is to realize
We are finally apart
Just where I want to be
To say I have moved on
And now I am free
So I ask you one last time
Why should I lie
The tears that you cried
Were your covered up lies
I have not an ounce of sadness within me for you
Knowing down deep this is my sweetness to the end
Saying goodbye is so easy to do
I will not shed a tear for you
I sit with my sigh of relief
Releasing myself from you in my life
To know there will be the true one for me
Who will love and care without a doubt
I embrace the fact
There is no going back
There is only this I know for sure
I'm fine without you

WHERE IS GOD

Where is God
You continue to ask
You continue to wonder
Open up your eyes
Open up your ears
God has always been here
Waiting for all of his children to come
Each and everyone
God has gone no where
He waits for you to cry out to him,
He knows your needs before you do
He knows what is best for you
So get on your knees and pray
Spend time with him
Get away from this noisy world
Watch how he will change
Your life for the good
So beautiful and true

THE MOURNING FOG

It can be so thick
With uncertainty
As you wonder what the meaning is
What it will do with you
What it will do for you
In what direction it will guide you in
And wonder if it will see you through to the end
You name it you give it life
Is it the loses of loved one
Is it the loses of your life story
Is it the emptiness within
Is it the heart broken so many times
Is it the cruel intentions of others
Is it the loses that should of stayed
Is it the lessons in your life that failed
Is it the fear that overcomes you sometimes
The doubt of who you are
The hate that surrounds you
The inflictions you welcome
As you ask yourself will it get better
As you ask will this confusion
 Finally create my understanding
Will the end appear will it be near to me
With all the necessary goodbyes
With all the unnecessary tears that you have cried
As you prepare for something new
You try to move it and do what you can with it
As it floods into your life into your soul
With this desperation covers every inch of your life
Without direction in sight
Only darkness covers your steps once again
Occupying your time and mind
With a world that is spinning out of control

Whatever whenever whoever
Sleep it's call the cure for all of it
Relief from the reality of this mourning fog
The brokenness you feel deep inside
That either makes you or breaks you not the same
As this war rages on inside
Then the victory of healing takes place
Never let go you tell yourself
Never give in you tell yourself
As the final victory approaches
As you breath a sigh of relief
Just when it all seems this is the end of you

MISSING LIFE

As we continue to surround ourselves
With the reality of a lost world
All this pressure and pain
Drives us to insanity in our thoughts
And what have we gained
We start to grasp at anything that does not move
Crushing our happiness completely
Leaving us with nothing
Except this emptiness that echoes in our mind
We look around us wanting everything around us
But the realization of it all
Will never give us the completeness of peace
We carry our past into our present once again
Waiting for yet another chapter of our lives to be the same
Doom gloom desperation engulfs our entire being
It plagues us in so many ways
We begin to loose sight of how to truly live
We cram all this unnecessary punishment on ourselves
Never stopping and taking a deep breath of relief
As the fearing this moment in time of opposition
Controls your mind in motion
As it slowly breaks you down
The impact just will not go away
The cruel words crumbling your spirit
The punishment of others is allowed without consent
The haunting continues to kill you slowly
You say you are in fear to die
But you die just to live your life
Your memory plays a rerun of what was
An awareness of the good will never be a part of you
But the mistakes play with you
Choking the life out of you
As you once again put yourself

In this unnecessary turmoil
Called your personal grief
Something that you hold onto so tightly
Is once again a cut so deep within
That you finally wake up feeling no pain

HATE SORROW PAIN (NOTE TO MY ABUSERS)

You are my abuser
My hate is my sorrow is my pain
What is your gain
What is your pleasure
To inflict the weak
A man whose name is known
A hated and despised person
That society did not want
Your hands that hurt our outer shell
Your words that cut deep within
Molding internal pain within us
A disguise of your coward self
The fear you inflict in our being
The shame you will know
A man you never were
The innocent ones consumed by your abuse
Many years of fear
As I kept it alive with my hate
A heart full of scars
A little girl
An innocent baby
We are stuck back in the past with you
As I slowly let go and forgive you now
You were full of demons
Only wanting to hurt and torment others
Who could not protect themselves
As we are continually being reminded once again
Who you were and always will be
Leaving all these wasted years where they belong
Wondering why you did what you did
Throwing you down a gutter no longer to be found
Your words a menace to your mouth

Your actions without emotions
As death comes upon you
I stand still with relief knowing
You will never hurt us again
As you suffer a unmerciful death
Of all the violence you inflicted onto others
As for me I am free now of you
Numb and empty inside
Emotions are non existing
As you eat your own abuse
Crying out for forgiveness
As you tried to destroy the innocent ones
One day you took your last breath
As the memories of you faded into the ground with you
A sense of peace within me knowing
You will never be spoken about again

SMILES

Those smiles into frowns
You live in such a dark place
Within your mind
As it consumes you everyday
Where did your happiness go
As I sit and watch with wonder
If anyone has this awareness now
Amongst all of these people that pass me by
As you exhibit your torment from inside
Is it a story untold
A broken spirit
Fear that engulfs your being
A feeling that no one cares
Is it lonely or despair
A heart that was broken so many times
An emptiness that echoes so loud
As you wish and hope it lifts
With regrets you wish would disappear
Self hate inflicted on ourselves by ourselves
Where is the love for you
It eats you from the inside out
This sickness comes in like a raging storm
Tossing us everywhere unknown
With no relief in sight
Was it a promise broken from another
Was it a wish that never came true
As you feel so many broken pieces inside
To many to put back together
Pain doubles you over at times
You want to quit but something that lives within
Pushes you forward to take a few more steps
To never give up only go on
Your smile that once was

Seems to be only a memory
The many faces that I see
Many forms of frowns
The smile that once was
Is now upside down

BACK TO MYSELF

A grown man
Was just my thought
Caring for you
Was like a real love unreal
Hopes and desires
Flaming fires
You crept your way towards my life so slowly
A relationship of perfect dysfunction
Abuse with a passive spin on it
Years of torment of pain
A lonely woman
Seeking not much but happiness
A significant other
Then the magic appears
Fogging my mind to the unrealistic of you
Secrets selfish motives self gratification
A few positives into the mountain of negatives
Lessons compiled into massiveness
Trying to dig my way of out of this hole of hell
A mere man who taught me well,
Like a lemon oh so sour but so sweet like sugar
A deep burning desire
Screams within me
Slow destruction eating away inside of me
Finally breaking from your bondage of dysfunction and deceit
Promises of the word never again
With a great push inside of me
Awaking so differently
Finding myself once again.
Her voice on my phone
Talking a whisper
A gratifying moment of your flesh
Positions and hungry loins

So much better to day than yesterday
Oh the evil laughter from your voice box of selfish deceit
A dirty porn movie was yours
With the words that spoke loudly in my ear
My vivid imagination of your sick and twisted self
Seeing it in my mind
Filled with euphoria of joy and happiness now
Knowing that the memory of you eliminated
Is the true companion of mine
Freedom has come to join me
Embracing the new lessons like a hug
No regrets despair or anger
Digging deep within my hurting heart that is healed
Leaving all the baggage behind
For you to finally carry your own
Is sweet success for me
No regrets only freedom from the bondage of you
Sitting no longer in this classroom
With the teacher
The small voice within
Speaking once again
Who is God that loves me unconditionally
Letting go was not my choice
But then again
Never to look back
Was the reality of letting go
Only to realize the need
To truly love myself completely
Expecting more for me
Finally walking the road
To where I am free

FISHING

Fishing is the calming sport of the human race
As we go on our merry way to catch something new
We wait contemplate and never forget
The reason why the worm made fishing possible
Off we go with box and fishing pole in hand
Down the road round the corner a bait store oh boy
We step inside to buy some little creatures of the dirt and dark side
They are our friendly friends we call worms
We carry them in a coffin box not dead yet
Struggling to find a way out wiggling to be set free
From the death sentence that soon will be
As we prepare the long slim fishing pole hook at the end
It all begins with the worm we call our friend
We pick the fattest and longest worm of all
Slowly bringing its demise
Never saying a word of thanks or goodbye
We place the worm so slowly onto the hook
As we prick our finger not realizing how painful it may be
On our new friend we call worm
On you go as you carefully slide this worm
So slowly placed onto the hook
As we hear no screams, words or squeak
Of pain from this poor little worm that hangs so helpless
Waiting to be eaten and die
Off you throw him into the water
As you wait in anticipation for that fish
To come along and eat your friend
Swallowing every inch of him
As you lift your fishing pole to see
Realizing there is nothing not even the worm called me
He died so quickly for his enemy the fishes meal
And you did not stop to thank him
For sparing his life so freely for you

MY DAUGHTER

Many years have passed
As life goes by quickly
Wasted years of foolishness
As I sit and wonder why
The many years I've cried
For God to stop you
And show you the way
You have made yourself a slave
To the choices you have made
All the bondage of torment you cause yourself
Makes me stop and wonder why
But then memory of the days gone by
I now understand and have moved on
As you continue to open yourself to the devils way
All this unnecessary infliction of sorrow and pain
As your children and mother wait for your wake up call
You call them opportunities I call them a wasted life
I ask God when will it end
As your mother and children pray for your salvation
As God continues to allow your choices
To the path to the unknown
God has saved you and protected you
From your own self destruction
And all your children and mother can do is wait once again
I know God loves you cause you are still around
Living your life so carelessly
Wake up and see how lucky you still are
Time is running out on your selfishness
Your children and mother sit in pain
For all the self torture you have done to yourself
You talk about death like it is a trophy to win
As you continue to sit and play with your sin
And all your children and your mother can do is wait on you

All the pain you have caused the innocent ones
We will never understand your decisions
You talk about them like there is nothing wrong
You inflict your attitude on others for all you have done
One day you may wake up too late
And all your children and mother can do
Is finally let you go and let God take over you
For when God finalizes a persons life
He can either take it away
Or make a testimony out of it
Your children and your mother has had their faith to get them through
No matter the outcome of what you do
You will realize this uncaring world you live in
Does not care about what happens to you
So there is one things I ask of God
Is it your time for a new beginning or the death of you

MY GRANDDAUGHTER AMYIAH

As I reflect on my life
I see God's love through you
You are a blessing to me in my life
This is for sure
I am so grateful for you
When God blessed my life with a special delivery to me
God put the perfect ingredients together who is you
All the love a grandmother could ever want and need
Your determination to succeed started before you were born
into this world
You are so beautiful
Molded so perfectly in God's image
When I see you my love overflows
My heart is touched with so much happiness inside
Your so very special to me my life is fulfilled
So when life gets me down and my heart is sad
I think of you Amyiah you make me happy
So just remember this in your life
When you need someone to be there for you
I will not be very far away
Your in my thoughts and in my prayers,
I ask God to always be there for you
To bless your life abundantly
To be there guiding your steps along the way
Make you always feel happy throughout your days
And protect you in life
Remember Amyiah all the love I have for you
As I thank God for you I want you to know
I could not of picked a more wonderful grand daughter
Than you for my life
You are so special to me

MY GRANDSON KELVIN JR.

You are my inspiration
My hopes and my dream
When God gave me you
I could not ask for more.
He put you together so perfectly
You are amazing to me
You have given me love unconditionally
Your handsome so brilliant
So caring and compassionate
Everything you do amazes me
You give me such a happiness in my heart
You fulfill the many voids of others
Your words of encouragement help me to go on
God chose someone special that is you
Your determination will bring you many places in life
Your many gifts will touch many in this life
To have you as my grandson
There are so many words to say about you
Jus how blessed I am to have you a part of my life
You are so special to me
And I hope you know that
I love you so much Kelvin
I will always be there you
No matter how hard life can get
Always remember I am with you always
You are in my thoughts and in my prayers everyday
I only want the best for you
God will protect and guide you in everyway
May your life be blessed abundantly
May your hearts desires come to fruition
You meant the world to me
I will always send you love your way
You are the best grandson
This grandmother could ever be blessed with

OUR EARTHLY MOM

She plants a seed
With the people she meets
Ministering to all
The love for those to keep
People in need know her well
She is a living example a story to tell
A woman who walks with Jesus by her side
A Sheppard of sorts to all the wandering souls
Begrudging no one accepting them all
When they begin to stumble begin to fall
She is there to catch them always
She carries their sorrow anguish pain and fear
Feeling it all as if it were hers
She gives hope to the hopeless
The lost found once again
Drying each tear showing them love
Just like God who lives up above
She hugs them all
With a familiar love they once knew in their lives
Teaching each one how to forgive themselves and others too
Treating each one like her own children,
Helping them along a road of many regrets
With no judgment only the love from a woman called mom to many
As time goes by and the years are present
When that day she is called back home to her loving God
She will stand in awe in front of Jesus
Hearing those final words
Welcome home my child
My good and faithful servant
The jobs that I gave you are well done
As she is greeted once again
By the many that have passed on
She touched while living on earth

ODE TO MENOPAUSE

Hear ye hear ye
It's finally here
The wonderful world of menopause
What an insidious word or so it seems
Bulges folds wrinkles and crinkles included
Snap crackle and pop goes the body too
My mood seems to plummet deep down inside
I think I want to cry get mad and run away too
But then I realize I am so confused
Patience anyone have extra for me
I huff and puff with all that stuff
Around my waist a muffin top
Specially ordered for me.
Acne it's a friend of mine
It has attached itself to my face for all to see
My eyesight seems ok
Darkness in the light seems so odd to me
My memory not to bad
Can't remember what I've had
Heartburn and gas my new hobby
I'm hungry again and have just eaten
Exercise a great past of mine
I think about it as time passes me by
Chin hair oh joy a moustache to match
Hot flashes seem so mild
When I am out in the snow
Aches and pains seem all the same
I think I want to go up in space
So gravity can pull up my body and face
My soul inside of me is a perfect 19 years of age
It wants to play but I'm just to tired now
Bathing suits and bikini's are a thing of the past
I'll sit in my tub just me myself and I

Full size moo moo's so comfy when the bloat arrives
Gray hairs just recently died
Spider veins and varicose veins what a deal
A turkey neck and Thanksgiving is not even here
Muscle tone jiggles skin so soft and has lost it's way
It's falling down and just don't want to stay
I refuse to sneeze or cough
These rolls not only at the bakery
Briefs my new bikini to wear
A girdle seems so obsolete
I think I'll bring it back how neat.
Marionette lines sound so royal on my face
When I look in the mirror no queen does appear
I see the places I have been in life
They are called the roads I have traveled around in circles
So I ask myself once again
Self what is this all about
And does it really matter
As I sit and contemplate with an answer to my question
This is my new found friend(s)
They will be called Ode to menopause just for me
As I once again sit and think about my life
And play once again

PRAISE THE LORD

Praise the Lord everyday
Praise the Lord in everyway
Praise the Lord for you Life
Praise the Lord for all your strife
Praise the Lord for all his love
Praise the Lord for all he gives
Praise the Lord for all he does
Praise the Lord for the path he leads you
Praise the Lord for he is the King.
Praise the Lord for he is here.
Praise the Lord for the skies above
Praise the Lord for he is in control
Praise the Lord and sing to him
Praise the Lord in loving him
Praise the Lord for he is good
Praise the Lord for all his blessings
Praise the Lord always

FAMILIAR KIND

I am the person that you see
I am the person that you hear
I am the person that is honest
I am the person who is kind
I am the person who is gentle
I am the person who is strong
I am the person who is real
I am the person who is brilliant
I am the person who is friendly
I am the person who is happy
I am the person who is funny
I am the person who has no fear
I am the person who is loving
I am the person who has great wisdom
I am the person who is truth
I am the person who is beautiful
I am the person who is giving
I am the person who is hopeful
I am the person who is tenacious
I am the person who is honest
I am the person who is sensitive
I am the person who is open
I am the person who does not quit
I am the person who is unique
I am the person who is compassionate
I am the person who is optimistic
I am the person who is romantic
I am the person who is independent
I am the person who is concerned
I am the person who makes the choice
I am the person with an opinion
I am the person who you see
I am the person who is brave

I am the person who she is
I am the person that speaks the truth
I am the person who has desires
I am the person who has dreams
I am the person of many chances
I am the person who has made mistakes
I am the person who does forgive
I am the person who does believe
I am the person who tolerates
I am the person who is a child of God
I am the person who loves her God

ARE YOU THERE GOD

I walk in darkness are you there God
My mountains so high are you there God
My valleys so low are you there God
A burning inside are you there God
I am sad are you there God
I am lost are you there God
I am in fear are you there God
I am in need are you there God
I am lonely are you there God
I am broken are you there God
I am desperate are you there God
I am depressed are you there God
I am so angry are you there God
I am hurt are you there God
I am confused are you there God
I am tired are you there God
I want to let go are you there God
I am suffering are you there God
I am in despair are you there God
I need a change are you there God
I need peace are you there God
I need love are you there God
I need happiness are you there God
I need completeness are you there God
I need contentment are you there God
I need fulfillment are you there God
I need you in everything are you there God
I am not sure if I believe are you there God
I do not feel your presence are you there God
Disconnected from God

MELTED YEARS

The just melt away
They seem so distant from me now
Many of them gone with memory
Placing a blank picture inside the mind
Wondering who or where are they now
A life that flee so easily
As each minute of each day are shorten breaths
As a new day dawns
A lost yesterday seems just now before me
As a walk forward in the newness of this day
Without any of the reflections of yesteryears
Of only the days gone by
The years that have melted away so fast on me
A memory of trauma desperation and sadness
Have made a home in my mind
As I recall the regrets resentment and bitterness
The anger rages on inside of me
Burning me with a cancer that eats me up inside
If only I could let go and go forward
Leaving all this past behind
Closing the doors of these melted years
That will finally disappear

GALLERY OF MY LIFE

Collection of memories
In a my memory
A motion picture
Playing it's reruns
They are the finest
Ones you would like to forget
Colorful pictures
All the negative ones
Spread out for one to see
Look at my pain
My true self exposed once again
One story
To many stories
Not one the same
Touching the souls that surround me
The changes I have felt
Timeless breathless emotionless
Standing tall always strong
No cracking no breaking only bending allowed
The heart pains hiding within
Wanting to know me
Can you see
Can you hear me
Can you feel me
You call me an uncertainty
Nothing seems simple
Only wasted time
Only wasted life
Only wasted truth
What you see in me
Is what you get for you
Take me
Leave me
Search for me once again

IMAGINE

There was only love
We accomplished our goals
If we spoke only positive words
If people smiled how contagious it would be
If we were positive all the time
If there was no sickness
If our emotions were neutral
If we put change in action
If we were kind to everyone
If we lived in peace
If we were grateful all the time
If there was no such thing as complaining
If violence ended
There was no heartache
If mean people were not around
If children did not pick up adult actions
If the word I can't did not affect us
If we lived our lives correctly
If your vulgar language was stuck in your mouth
If your true thoughts were heard
If we walked forward in our lives
We stopped living in the past
If we loved our selves more
If mean words went back on the person saying them
There was no man made wars
Imagine if there was no fear
Imagine if there was only happiness
There was no greed
There was no poverty
If everyone shared with one another
If people spoke the truth
If work was the same as fun
Everyone took time to care for the earth

If evilness never existed
If we took time to pray more
If we spent more time with God
If everyone believed in God

WWJD

When you want to give up
When you want to give in
When you want to inflict revenge
When you want to destroy others
When you want to see suffering
When you want to do evil things
When you want to take things that are not yours
When you want to hoard your riches
When you want to torment the innocent one
When you want to abandon your role as a parent
When your cruel intentions affected someone badly
When all your words are nothing like your deeds
When you constantly lie to many who you truly are
When you are deceitful too many times
When you do not care only about yourself
When your words you spoke came true
When your words impacted someone for the rest of their lives
When your lies were now your truth
When your inflictions onto others came back on you
When what is wrong is right
When what is right is wrong
When your abuse is what is your problem
When you swallow down your pain
When you never walked forward into the unknown
When all your belief in God was gone
WWJD

ACCEPTANCE

Causes of gain
Causes of happiness
Causes of sadness
Causes of hope
Causes of fear
Causes of pain
Causes of loss
Causes of change
Causes of patience
Causes of healing
Causes of moving on
Causes of faith
Causes of submission
Causes of relief
Causes of release
Causes of abundance
Causes of goodness
Causes of peace
Causes of reassurance
Causes of confidence
Causes of belief
Causes of surrender
Causes of letting go
Causes of letting God
Causes of prayer

NEVER ENDING

The chain reaction
To compassion
Love that surfaces
Evil resurfaces
Trying to put out the light
That is so bright
This dark and dying world
Affected and defected
Shattered and broken
Desperation and hopelessness
Hate and evilness
The condition of the heart
Was and always will be
Filled with the human condition
As God's army goes forward
To defeat and destroy the destruction
As it marches forward into a war zone

BETRAYAL

A friend
An enemy within
Your dark evil colors
Showing through to me
Your lies and deceit
Your self destructive actions
The finger that points
Three back at you
Your hurtful words
Cuts deep within me
That echoes in my ears
Is finally a memory
I choose to forget
As I embrace your exit
Out of my life
The void of you
Is the relief I finally know and feel
That you no longer exist
As a part of my life
Your own words and actions
Is the karma that will haunt you
Is the karma that will consume you
By these cruel infested words and actions
You attempted to inflict on me
This realization of who you are
For all the world to see
Is the fakeness of your own belief
Of who you always were and will be
But hid it not so well with the words of your thoughts
Of others that you destroy in private
The guilt you have felt and will continue to feel
Will have a name on it who is me
For you will never be a part of my life
What a peaceful thought for me

DESTINATION

If only in my mind
A true love
Or a long stretch of time
As my memory fades
To my own fantasy
With these strange feeling
I call my own
A short duration s
Of echoing emptiness
Deep inside of me
Calls the truth
That is that reality of mine
That fools me
With this realization
Once again
That my senses
Of this figment
To my reality
Is the vivid images
Of my deceiving thoughts
Of what reality was
That never came true

Raging War of You

Being caught in your lies
Some you encounter will know
The trueness of you
Your worth and your truth
Will attach itself to your loss
As you attempt to tell me
What I want to hear
What I want to feel
As I continue to feel your lies
With a final goodbye
I hand down to you
As my silence towards you
Will deafen your mind with my words
As I inventory my life once again
Contemplating what to keep
Contemplating what to let go of
That will leave me with alight load
Of goodness and wholeness
With out you

OWN IT

My hurt
Is my pain
My anger
Is you
We choose our poison
In this life we decide
If this is going to
Eat us alive
Or will we defeat it
Before it kills our being
Allowing it to
Devour us slowly
Letting it dine
And the devil that is behind you
Taking your mind
Never cleaning it up
Only leaving it messy
For you to try to
Find your way out of it
As the mark of the devil
Kills you with scars

INNOCENT CHILD

A parent and a child
A mixture of both
Look through their eyes
And you will see
Yourself and your past
Staring back at you
Their fear is real
Your fear is real
Look through their eyes
They are your eyes too
This darkness inflicted upon them upon you
Running from the unknown as you run too
Of what you continue to do to them
And what they continued to do to you
They are numb inside and you are too
As they swallow and you swallow
Once again this numbness deep down inside
Self infliction yours and theirs
They are not allowed to feel neither are you
They are not allowed to speak neither are you
And there you are there they are
Once again in front of both of you
Your parent and a child that is you
That vicious cycle that continues to be created
Where it never stops
As it continues to be created once again
The ways that were taught to you
You teach them the same
The pain that you felt and pushed down
They do the same
Swallowing your fire of cancer
As they swallow the fire of cancer too
That never leaves

As you do the same
To that innocent child that is in that mirror with you
That stands in front of you
With tears in their eyes
Fear beyond their tears
There you are many years later
You continue to inflict them with
That pain that is your claim
Of your past with that parent(s)
As you once again leave
Another mess of what
Is wrong with you
Onto the innocent child
And this world needs to stop
Corrupting and staining our children now

(UN) COMFORTABLE ZONE

A comfort zone
Will continue to serve us
With a stuck zone that
Will eventually be
Our (un) comfortable zone
Then we will be forced
To confront and fight
To either move on
Or stay stuck
In this same zone of dying
Let us partake
Let us move on
To an unknown life
To embrace this graduation
To the new
For if we do not
We will never partake
In the newness of blessings
That wait our arrival
As the universe
Stands quietly with patience
For our fulfillment

WHAT IS

Incompleteness of you
Incompleteness of me
Now we have incompleteness of me
Filled with emptiness
Filled with pain
Filled with insanity
Filled with this emptiness
Filled with this loneliness
Filled with confusion
A hunger that cannot be fulfillment
Detached and attached
These wrong reasons to my reasons
No completeness
Go on now
Stay now
No turning back
Back to my pain
Unworthy
Self hate
Save myself
Drowning myself
All this heartache
From this brokenness
Once again
Can't fix you
Can't fix me
Self infliction
Is all we see
Comfortable dysfunction

YEARS OF SEASONS

Years of seasons in my life
Trudging through the pain
Trudging through more pain
Trudging through the worse pain
Trudging through the unending pain
Losing life losing breath
A self torment to myself continues
As I continue to carry the many types of baggage
Heart crushing heart breaking heart cracking
Drowning in this despair I continue to wade through
Living in this mind of hell
Attracting all the same in different forms
Of others who continue to walk down
A familiar path to the past
Waiting for the seasons of my life to change
Waiting for the seasons of my life to transform me
Looking in this mirror of reruns
Holding onto the what use to be
Making it once again new to me
Wasting so much time in life
With the others who do not change

COME

To me
        In me
                Through me
                        LORD
This victory
        Has
                Just begun
                        For me
As
        The decay
                Of delay
                        Is your plan
For my
        Personal progress
                AMEN

AS FOR ME

Procrastination
Is the assassination of motivation
To die to self
Is to live again
The empty pursuits
Is this plenty to poverty
God's control
Is the green light to life
Impact of negativity
Is the internal chatter of nothingness
As this continues in my perseverance
The power of this never ending tenacity within me
Fighting the invisible evilness
That lays dormant in front of me
A spiritual war begins to rage once again
This blindness is unnoticeable and never seen
Grabbing onto this fear base anxiety
Crushing it's throat with the suffocation of death
Knowing this new war will never survive
Knowing this war will never win
That this defeat will be a sweet victory
As for me

WALKING ON

One more critical path I walk
Bring the only true self who is me
The darkness of this world
Attempted to consume me so many times
Trying to minimize my whole being
To many pieces
I continued to walk forward
I continued to walk through
To the unknown storms
As they spun out of control
Tossing me around
Without any concern
No help to be found
Compassion was just a hell for me
As I wondered where I would land
Then this silence of peace
Appeared and there you were
I was right in the palm
Of my Father God's hand always
Every step of the way he kept me safe
Every step of the way he kept me strong
Every step he carried me on
Showed me his mercy and grace
The final light so bright
Took down the darkness that tried to destroy me

HOLDING ON

I hold onto me
Holding onto you
Not a word
Not a touch
Then I sink
Into a lonely reality
Will it
Will it not
Hoping
Wishing
Wanting
Waiting
Burning with desire
Feeling the pain
Facing the reality of not the same
How long
Will you be mine
Wishing that the picture I had for us
Would of never changed
And stayed the same an eternity
As the sinking in my heart
Echoes the voice
It never ever was and never will be
As the fantasy rushes through me
Standing in this once again
Do you feel the burn
Will you ever feel the burn
As I attempt to set my self free
Into this reality
Alone once again
Allowing it to fade away
To this nothing that always was

NEVER DOUBT

A critical path
Back to my true self
When the darkness of this world
Attempts to consume me
My whole being shaking
As I walk through the unknowns storms
Of my life spinning out of control
Causes confusion and fear
Tossing me around without direction
Showing no mercy or compassion
Then this silence of peace
Embraced me with a sense of relief
Knowing my Father my God
Was with me all along
In the palm of his hand of protection
Keeping me safe from destruction of the devil
Saving me with his grace and mercy
And unconditional love
Staying strong carrying on
With God I will keep on keeping on
With perseverance I will not give up
With the wisdom I will not give in
I will never abandon the ship
For God is continually
Directing my life for the good

MOVEMENT

Being uncomfortable in my pain
Forces me to face this struggle
It pushes me forward to grow
In my life once again
The thorn(s) have names
The thorn(s) keep my past alive within me
As I take another deep breath
As the tears flow like a current of water
Going down a stream
I stop to turn around
To embrace my realization
That the time has come to let go and let God
Digging down deep inside of me
Where all this pain has lived for years
Wasting my years of precious life
Eating me uncontrollably inside
Causing this sickness that never leaves
Making the darkness consume me in my mind
Then a breath is taken
A sigh of relief makes it's appearance in front of me
You hugged me Lord with your arms
You kissed me Lord with your words
You surrounded me in your peace
That surpasses all understanding

FLOW OF LIFE

Flow of life a question about me
This new direction of myself
Being pulled pushed tossed up down and all around
A change has taken the place of unchanged
Knowing for sure it is God and not myself
The spirit of true discernment within me lives
Speaking slowly softly louder it becomes to me
This darkness of fear
I do not comprehend with understanding
A feeling of deafness
A feeling of blindness
Now visiting my life without an invitation
I sit wait trust in this spirit
Instructing me with steps of travel
Has the right time arrived
Is it time for the movements of go forward march ahead
To experience the next phase of this life my life
Knowing that I will be leaving
All the yesterday years behind me
These types comforting me
This unknown time in my life
Hearing the reassurance
As God instructs this new path
That I must take and experience now
All that I can say is what appears in front of me
To be the flow of my life now

UNCERTAINTY

This question is why
This black hole still here
Blindness over comes me
Confusion scurries along
Attempting to attach itself onto me
Or so it seems
As I walk so carefully
With loud steps 1- 2- 3
Letting it know who I truly em
I go deeper and deeper
Feelings of all the mixed up emotions
That I continue to embrace
Attempting to toss them up
Letting them go
Fall as they may
Taking a deep breath of relief
Urgency is the moans this world cannot hear from me
A vision comes a glimmer of hope
A presence of familiarity surrounds me
As the war continues to the things
That does not belong any longer with me
As I shake it off
Vowing to myself to carry on
As my spirit will never be destroyed
By this uncertainty

JUST ME

My worth
Never mattered much
Your assumption of who I am
Your expectation of me
Was created by your ignorance
As you continue to inflict me
With your self worth of who you are
My self worth is so powerful
Not a reflection of your worth to me
Not a reflection of your words onto me
As your tongue is this weapon
That tries to cut me and take me down
But turns back onto you
There is a better me
There is a bigger me
There is a stronger me now
Than what you were towards me
Your mouth filled with worthless words
As your darkness attacks you
And my light over rides you
As I celebrate the end to this error

REALITY

These struggles in life
Seem like all you can do
Is face the front of it
With your blindness called pain
We travel the familiar path
Once again floundering and contemplating
When will it end
When do I surrender myself to it all
Do I torture myself and continue
As my heart loses it place
Holding the many sections in my hand
Hoping it will not drop and splatter
With my broken wants needs desires and dreams
You hate it and hate it once again
Overwhelmed with going on or staying
In the same place you run from
Turmoil has attached it self to you
It has relocated with my permission
Holding onto a glimmer of hope
Called God
Waking up entirely a different person
Looking back to the past I created
Wondering why it took so long
To let it go
This is called my death
A trade from pain to total peace
Incompleteness to wholeness
Sadness to happiness
Desperation to inspiration

ANGLE IT

My anger turns into my rage
Distraught with oppression
With a numbness of disbelief
This emptiness leaves me
Mentally
Emotionally
Spiritually depleted
The guilty failings
That leaves one
Exasperated and breathless
With a confusion of the unknown
As fear fills itself with darkness
Pain is this discord
Defeat is the end to my surrender
Turmoil forces change
As our resentments are now released

CHILDHOOD MEMORY

Rainbow of colors
Radiator and crayons
Beautiful and amazing
Melting downward from upward
Melting from long to short
Disappearing in front of me
My imagination was my creation
To my fascination
Wanting to see my crayons disappear
Into these many spectacular different colors
Running into this embracing love
Of my innocent reality of curiosity
A wonderful colorful childhood memory
Of this picture perfect creation
That is for me and created by me
Of a life of simplicity
That once was mine

WHAT I SEE

Silent suffering everywhere
It eats you up inside
Taking away every ounce
Of your life and happiness
Desperation consumes you
As you attempt to smile
The outside is so deceiving
But inside you die
All that is done at times
Is the picking up of the same broken pieces
We attempted to toss away
Putting them back in a different way
Asking if they can go in backwards
Where reality once again will be fine
But in your mind
You know you are still broken
Living in your broken life
Walking through this broken world
Not alone

MY ADDICT

What you do to you
You do to me
When you love that person
Who is an addict
They are not the only ones
That is affected by this dis-ease
It is called addiction
With it's many forms
We are all affected
By this addiction of the addict
We become addicted by the addiction
In our minds as well
Most of the time
If not all of the time
We may experience the addict
Recovered and appear healed
We are still addicted
To the fear that the addict will
Relapse overdose and die anyways
Now we are left addicted to the addict
With our own addiction why

CARRY ON

So much sadness in this world
Spinning out of control
Struggling to survive
On the edge I sit
Trying to take one more breath
Racing thoughts
Craziness
Silence
Darkness
Irrational thinking
Going in the wrong direction of this madness
Pondering when it will stop
When death comes upon me
Then I wait and stop to think
The decisions I have made
The things I have done
The realization of how lucky I am
To still be alive
To stop and thank God one more time
But then me the fool
Does it all over again

MEMORIES OF LIFE

My life
Differently formed and molded
Darkness into light
Unexpected to the expected
Uncertain to the certain
Pain into healing
Fear into courage
Weakness into strength
Doubt into belief
Confusion into understanding
Bondage into freedom
Mountains into hills
Hills into valleys
Valleys into cliffs
Cliffs into clarity
All is well with God

SHOULD I

Chance it
Change it
Embrace it
Run from it
Examine it
Reject it
Dissect it
Yes it
No it
Trust it
Fear it
Love it
Demand of it
Judge it
Care for it
Pull it apart
Put back together
Reinvent it
Leave it alone
Ignore it
Accept it
Shun it
Follow it
Walk away from it
Support it
Let it go

ABSENTEE LIFE

What do we miss each day
The wind that blows on our face
The many people we pass by
The smile someone gives to us
The love we need to give to others
The birds that sing a song for us
The dog that stops to be patted
The trees that give us shade
The food we eat
The drink we drank
The laughter we shared
The peace we feel if just for a moment
The next breath we take
The many blessings we have been given
The love God gives us so freely
What is it that we miss
While we stay in this turmoil
We call life

NEW YEAR

Its here
Old baggage
Same self
No dreams
Plummeting
    Down
        Once again
            In your life
                I am that failure

BROKEN HEART

My broken heart
My crying heart
Screams with pain
Someone mend me
Love me
Embrace me
Stop this hurt
Within my heart
Beating
Bleeding
Breaking
Eventual death comes silently
And it all stops forever

SOMETHING TO PONDER

How many times
Has God spoken to us
How many times
Have we listened to God
How many times
Have we ignored God
How many times
Have we prayed when things are good
How many times
Have we prayed when things are bad
How many times
Has God given us mercy
How many times
Have we sacrificed something to God
How many times
Has God given us grace
How many times
Has God blessed our lives
How many times
Have we truly trusted God
How many times
Have we spent time with God
How many times
Have we told God how grateful we are
How many times
Have we told God we love him
How many times
We have sacrificed for God
How many times
Have we totally relied on God
How many times
Have we doubted there is a God
How many times

TRAVELING POET

Traveling poet
This is what I am
My thoughts
My voice
My miracle pen
So much to say
My life an open book
My eyes have seen
My ears have heard
So many actions and words
A song
Of love
Of heartache
Some pain
Of anger
Of fear
Of hopes
And dreams
Of happiness
Of sadness
My mourning
My doubts
Bad choices
Some regrets
Loses included
All too familiar to me
Many blessings
From God above
As I speak to this world
Of brokenness
Of shame
Of hate
Trying to touch many lives
With my many words
Of
Poetry

REGRETS

The mistakes I have made
Have haunted me a lifetime
Through my thoughts and dreams
Of who you are
Of who you were to me
These regrets are like a death
That will never be resurrected
I hold onto hoping
With the many broken pieces
My desires are now shattered
Scattered memories of my actions
Haunts me
Shakes my soul
I cannot let go
I cannot move forward
You will always be my suffering
Through my words and actions
I am the only one holding this broken heart of mine
That never seems to leave me
As it lays dormant once again
Waiting to rise up once again
With the unmerciful reminder
That you will always consume my life
With your name attached to it (JW)

TRANSPARENT

I speak loud
I speak with my pain
I speak with my feelings
I speak with my infliction(s)
I speak with my abuse
I speak with my fear(s)
I speak with my anger
I speak with my trigger(s)
I speak with my torment(s)
I speak with my confusion
I speak my doubt(s)
I speak with my mind
I speak with my chaos
I speak with my voices
I speak with my past
I speak with my present
I speak with my future
I speak with my hope(s)
I speak with my self
It screams to come out
I speak my next breath
As I become breathless once again

THE OTHER SIDE

A dream
    A thought
        A sense
            A smell
                A sound
                    A sign
                        You are around
                            Grasping it all now

MY WOMAN FRIEND(S)

(A dedication to all my woman friends)
She is unique indeed
Wisdom is a friend of hers
Freely sharing with others
She is that special woman
A daughter
A sister
A mother
A grandmother
A wife
A friend
She is a gift from God
With the many blessings she shares with many
Her caring heart includes a gentle soul
All who know her carry the many memories of her
Her smile bright as the sun
Her outer beauty is the reflection from within
Always making others feel welcomed
She is kind, patient and compassionate
Her loving and gentle ways takes the pain away
She is always sharing herself fully
Laughter is her antidote to many
She specializes in freely giving it to everyone
Never expects anything in return
She holds many close to her heart
The world is a much better place
I thank God for you
And for your friendship

TO YOU FROM ME

My time has come
The end to the old familiar me
A new beginning just for me
I have waited and anticipated
For this new change who is me
Many doors have opened
Many necessary doors have closed
All these choices I will finally embrace
Never to sit back and contemplate
My life my past will always be a part of me
But no longer me
My days will be different now
As I walk in my new freedom
Of happiness and hope
This new presence of me now
Is what I have waited for
I will reveal my true self to many
All the impact others left on me
Are the many lessons that will be my victory
My hope is to leave this world a better place
Leave my footprints on the heart of many
And to thank all the ones
Who made a difference in my life
In my life

JUST BELIEVE

A still small voice within
Do you hear it
Do you feel it
Do you believe it
Call it what you may
The noise and interruptions
Talk over it many times
A movement deep inside
A spirit a Holy Spirit
No just God
Directing your steps in life
Some call it a figment of imagination
No just God
Do you ignore it
As you sit in the stillness of this quietness
It once again calls out
Attempting to get your attention
As your mind races once again
This spirit within speaks so loud so clear
As you once again contemplate
Not giving a chance to the choice
Is it real

CARRY ON

Will I survive
You will survive
Will I hold on
You will hold on
God will provide
Has he no
Why all this worry
All in your head
It speaks the words of dread
Your mind tells you your going crazy
Stop wait and listen
Your inner spirit has a message
Just for you
It is the spirit of God
Talking to you
Carry on my child
Never give up
You future has plans
To prosper you not destroy you
For I am her with you always

CHAIN PAIN

My chain gets heavy
My chain called my bondage
My chain represent me
My chain many names on it
My chain makes me weary
My chain gives me fear
My chain wears me down
My chain is my anger
My chain is my pain
My chain is to give up
My chain is to give in
My chain is too heavy
My chain needs to go
My chain is letting go
My chain is breaking apart
My chain is no longer my chain
My chain has changed
Thank you Jesus

O COMFORT ZONE

O' comfort zone
Don't do this
Don't do that
Don't even try
Why
It never is going be
Leave it alone
All my fear
Freezes up inside
As it stops my process
Won't let my progress go forward
Try something new
The fear surrounds me now
O' comfort zone
I guess I will never try
I guess I will never know
Success
What will be
What could be
For me
Could of been
Should of been
As I stop myself
Once again
Moving on into the known
O' comfort zone
Not a worry you see
I will stay in my
O' comfort zone
It will be fine with me

CHANCE

What is this chance
Who took this chance
Will I be this chance
Are you this chance
Do you see chance
To do this chance
Stopping the chance
Letting go of this chance
What does it take to make a chance
What does it take to try a chance
Will it be another failed chance
Or will I try this chance
I'm going to take this chance

VICTIM NO MORE

I was your victim
Can't you see
A prisoner of your cell
I now forgive you
All is well
I no longer accept
The who you were
The what you did
I can finally face you
I can finally speak my peace
I will always remind you silently
Of the impact you left on me
I can finally tell you
What I really think
I will no longer hold back
I never broke
Like you wished
Just want to say
Thank you for my life
All this success
I am finally free from you
After all these wasted years on you
You no longer control me
Through my thoughts
You no longer control me
Through my emotions
You no longer control me
Through your words
I am that woman you violated
That has now moved on
To a new life I now live
But you will always be reminded
What you did to me
Sincerely karma

THINK TWICE

A dirty dish
Food to eat
A covered body
Clothes to wear
No broken feet
Shoes to wear
A time to sleep
A bed to lay in
Protection from storms
A house to live in
Money to spend
A job to go to
Speak you mind
Freedom of speech
People you love
Called a family
Count your blessings
Before it's all gone
I am grateful

MY BEATING HEART

For you
2 back to 1
Fast
Slow
Fast
Slow
Welling up inside
Emptiness echoes loudly
Brokenness
Loneliness
Mending
Healed
Letting go
Surrendering completely
Peace at last
Discovery of a new love
1 Single moment
Me

RERUNS

2 steps forward
3 steps back
Once again
Same issues
Hit the wall
Can't understand
Won't understand
Old tapes
Product of my past
Not good enough
Not confidence enough
No I can't
No I won't
Stay stuck
Seeking
Seeking
Seeking once again
To the unknown
Praying
Pleading
Praying
Pleading
In due time
I will

WHAT IS

The Lord is my peace
The world is a war zone
The Lord is my strength
The world is weakness
The Lord in my love
The world is hate
The Lord is my patience
The world is too fast
The Lord is my rock
The world is quicksand
The Lord is my certainty
The world is confusion
The Lord is my change
The world is the same
The Lord is my everything
The world is nothing
God is the end

SELF DESTRUCTION

This path I walk
Filled with destruction
Walking on my way
Fear erodes my soul
Numbness my best friend
Confusion to embrace
Self hate engulfs me
Failure haunts my mind
Talking and pointing the way
Desperation for relief
A toxic mix of death
Crack Heroin A pill
A smoke No sleep
Lethal injections
Hoping with wonder
Waiting with eyes wide open
A new day once again for me
Onto another path of destruction
This time goes slowly
Eats me inside everyday
This all to familiar
Give up Give in
Self pity Worry
Anger Defeat
Self hate Nothing more
Failure I feel this I know
I look into the mirror
With this stranger looking back at me
Nothing I recognize
Not even me
A slow suicide
A slow death of self
Lost time day years
My life a blur
A memory of forgetfulness
A reminder to my family
That I left behind
To suffer with me
Every step of the way
This is my self destruction
For everyone to see

BORROWED TIME

Did you ever borrow time
Did you ever really think
How much time
When is it time
Is it my time
Have I lost time
Where is time going
Will my time end
The we continue
We breathe
We smile
We laugh
We cry
We wonder
We hope
We reflect
We remember
We stop
We know
We look
We feel
We listen
We hear
We hope
We slow down
We stop
We realize
We are all on short time
We are all on borrowed time

MIDLIFE

My time of change
Of loss
Of gain
To love
To give
To know
To live
To face a new journey
To really try
To take a chance
To say goodbye
To challenge uncertainty
To exercise my strength
To show my confidence
To know my inner beauty
To use my voice
To speak the truth
To express who I am
To know the true me
To live simply
To be certain
To let go
To let God

WE ARE

We are all people
Of all colors
Of all nations
We are family
We are neighbors
We are friends
We have feelings
We have emotions
Our up bringing includes dysfunctions
We have hopes
We have dreams
We have desires
Our fears are deep
Our struggles real
Our determination is defeated
We are enemies
Killing ourselves
Destroying our future
Put away this hate
Let us UNITE

PRAISE YOU GOD

I want to praise you God
For all you do
I love you
I want to praise you God
Your so good to me
You have set me free
I want to praise you God
For the rest of my life
Because you made it right
I want to praise you God
You have given me great peace
And all my guilt is now released
I want to praise you God
And tell the world about you
You are my everything
I want to praise you God
You are my king
You make my heart sing
I want to praise you God
For all you have done
Cause you are the only one
I want to praise you God
More and more
For opening many doors
I want to praise you God
Forever and ever
Because you leave me never
I want to praise you God

CPSIA information can be obtained
at www.ICGtesting.com
Printed in the USA
FFOW03n1908060317
33162FF